WOMEN HEROES OF WORLD WAR I

///

To Shobha
Happy Birthday
Jan 20, 2017
Dany and Cindy

OTHER BOOKS IN THE
WOMEN OF ACTION SERIES

WOMEN HEROES OF WORLD WAR I

16 Remarkable Resisters, Soldiers, Spies, and Medics

KATHRYN J. ATWOOD

CHICAGO
REVIEW
PRESS

The Library of Congress has cataloged the hardcover edition as follows:

Atwood, Kathryn J.
  Women heroes of World War I : 16 remarkable resisters, soldiers, spies, and medics / Kathryn J. Atwood.
    pages cm
  Includes bibliographical references and index.
  ISBN 978-1-61374-686-8 (cloth)
  1. World War, 1914-1918—Participation, Female—Europe 2. World War, 1914-1918—Women—Europe—Biography. 3. World War, 1914-1918—Participation, Female—United States. 4. World War, 1914-1918—Women—United States—Biography. I. Title.

D639.W7A88 2014
940.3082—dc23

2013047408

Cover and interior design: Sarah Olson
Front cover photos: (top) Nurses in the Canadian Army Medical Corps, George Metcalf Archival Collection, © Canadian War Museum; (bottom, left to right) Elsie Inglis, *Dr. Elsie Inglis* (1919); Edith Cavell, St. Mary's Church, Swardeston, Norfolk, United Kingdom; Marthe Cnockaert, *I Was a Spy!* (1934); Ecaterina Teodoroiu, National Military Museum, Romania

Printed in the United States of America
5 4 3 2 1

To the men and women who lost their lives in the Great War.

"In valour, devotion to duty, and courage in the face of the enemy they were rated as soldiers by the soldiers themselves."

—British Major Thomas Coulson on female Allied agents

"I do not feel that I did anything exceptional. Any well girl can do the same."

—Arno Dosch-Fleurot, member of the Russian Women's Battalion of Death

CONTENTS

//

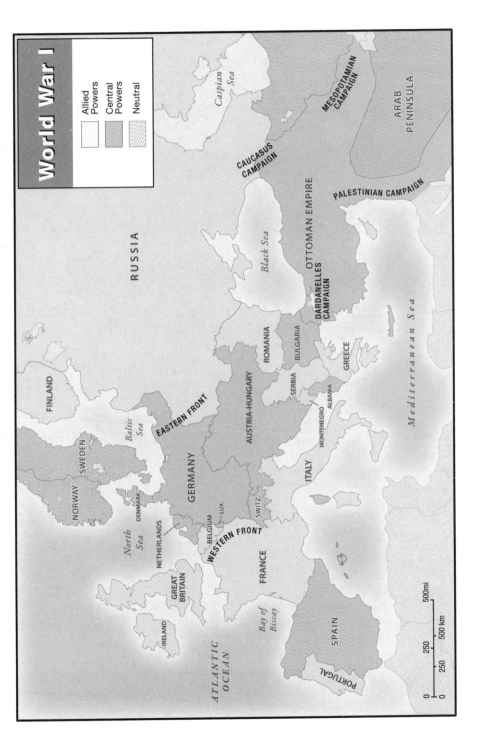

INTRODUCTION

///

When considering World War I, the images that generally come to the minds of most 21st-century people are few: soldiers wearing gas masks standing in sandbagged trenches or the smiling Archduke Franz Ferdinand and his wife just before they were assassinated. The connection between these images is generally unclear and most of the war's other details seem to belong in old, dusty history books—complex, remote, and dull—and not nearly as interesting as those regarding the world conflict that followed a few decades later.

But the fact is that World War I—or the Great War, as it was called at the time—was *the* most significant event in human history up to that point. It was one generation's great adventure-turned-nightmare that became the most cataclysmic event of the century, a war that destroyed the ideals of the 19th century and thrust the world violently into the 20th.

Yet when it began in August 1914, the First World War was greeted with enthusiasm on a scale that is nearly impossible for modern readers to fully comprehend.

"To-day has been far too exciting to enable me to feel at all like sleep—in fact it is one of the most thrilling I have ever lived through, though without doubt there are many more to come. That which has been so long anticipated by some & scoffed at by others has come to pass at last—Armageddon [epic battle] in Europe!"

—Vera Brittain, a young British woman,
diary entry for August 3, 1914

Why this excitement? An intense nationalism had been on the rise in Europe for several decades, and many saw the war as an opportunity to prove the greatness and preeminence of their particular countries. Most young people in the combatant nations had been instilled with the principles of honor, duty, and courage as well as a sense that those ideals were directly connected to a defense of their homelands and cultures. They were also taught very clearly who they should look upon as their country's particular enemy: for the French it was the Germans; for the Germans it was the Russians and the French; for the Russians it was the Germans and the Japanese. For the British it was anyone who would dare to challenge their global dominance.

Years before the war, many countries had encouraged semimilitaristic training for young men in order to make very clear the connection between nationalistic ideals and military service. And when the Olympic Games were revived on an international level in 1896—including 14 participating nations, 11 of them from Europe—it reinforced a strong connection between athleticism and nationalism. Pierre de Coubertin, the French man most responsible for the 1896 Olympics, had in the years prior promoted athletic training of French schoolchildren with the idea that athletes would be better soldiers.

Australian troops heading to the front, most likely early in the war.
Great War Primary Document Archive

When the war began in the late summer of 1914, it was as if the conflict represented, to the world's young men especially, the opportunity to participate in an Olympics. Only for this competition it was not a specifically mastered athletic skill that would allow one to participate; the only requirement—outside of some military training—was patriotism and the courage necessary to implement it.

"Men whose mobilization sheet bore a later date, envious of those who were called up immediately, chafed with impatience, and did all in their power to get themselves accepted at once."

—Louise Thuliez, French resister

So when their countries went to war, young men all over the world, no matter what their social status, left jobs, universities, and promising careers to join their nations' armed forces, thrilled that they would at last have an opportunity to put their ideals into practice. It was for many the fulfillment of a dream, the culmination of their greatest hope.

"We are elated beyond words. We too, in our small way are to help the country's cause."

—Florence Farmborough, British tutor living in Russia at the war's outbreak, on learning that she and her friends had been accepted by the Russian Red Cross as volunteer nurse aides

---

When the war first began, the majority of Europeans believed it would be over by the end of the year. But the only peace that occurred at that time was a temporary Christmas truce initiated by many fighting men on the western front; the war didn't end until late 1918. One of the many reasons it lasted so much longer than expected was that both sides on several fronts of the war were often fairly well matched, making it very difficult for one side or the other to gain enough of an advantage to win. As soon as thousands were killed, thousands more volunteered—or were conscripted—to take their place. The armies of World War I were huge; the total number of mobilized men reached far into the millions. Many of these men had left civilian work behind them. Who would replace them? For the most part, it would be women.

WOMEN AND WORLD WAR I

The war's powerful effect on women and their position at its outbreak can be seen clearly in the life of Vera Brittain, a young, upper-middle-class British woman who would become famous years later for her wartime memoir, *Testament of Youth*.

Vera had argued endlessly with her father regarding her desire to attend college. He couldn't understand why she didn't focus on finding a husband instead. She finally got her way in the fall of 1914 and began attending Somerville, a women's college that was part of Oxford.

"In those days it was a terrible thing for one's daughters to insist on having professions."

—Helena Gleichen, professional British artist
who worked as a radiographer during the war

But after a year of study, Vera dropped out in order to become a Voluntary Aid Detachment nurse. Why? University studies— much as she loved them—suddenly seemed too easy a vocation when Great Britain was at war. And more important, her fiancé, Roland Leighton, had postponed a promising Oxford career in order to join the military. Vera couldn't bear to be any less committed to the war effort than he was.

"I was adamant in my desire to go. . . . Our boys were donning Khaki. Everyone was bursting with pride in our nation, and I was as affected by this patriotic fervour as anyone else."

—Katherine M. Wilson-Simmie, Canadian nurse

Vera Brittain's choice to attend a relatively new women's university (Somerville had been established in 1879) reveals that opportunities and choices had been slowly growing for women of certain social classes. But her decision to switch to volunteer nursing and the relative ease with which she was able to take that opportunity demonstrate the powerful influences of both war-related propaganda and emotional connections to loved ones in the military *and* the new roles that the war suddenly made available to women.

Most women, like Vera Brittain, were eager to do their part in the war, and the governments of most combatant countries took advantage of this enthusiasm—some immediately and some more slowly. To keep things running on the home front, some governments officially encouraged women to step into civilian occupations made available by the manpower shortage.

German street car conductor during the war.
Germany in Wartime (1917)

"The [German] women were doing almost everything that the men had done."

—Josephine Therese, young American woman in wartime Germany

Italian women making fuses in a munitions factory. *Courtesy Allison Scardino Belzer, from* La guerra: dalle raccolte del reparto fotografico del Comando supremo del R. esercito, *vol. 9 (1917)*

Women who wanted work that felt more directly related to the war, and who could afford to work without pay, quickly filled new volunteer positions within the medical services. Those who had similar motivations but depended on their paychecks were encouraged to work in munitions factories (usually making more money than they could elsewhere), making not only weapons and ammunition but also war-related products that hadn't previously been mass-produced, such as periscopes, binoculars, and airplanes.

To be considered officially useful outside the realm of normally accepted women's work was very exciting for many of the women who now became active in supporting their countries' war efforts. And some of them could see further possibilities in all of it.

"While the Italian country man . . . fought . . . the Italian country woman worked the land as if she were a man."

—Matilde Serao, Italian journalist

Many of the women involved in the decades-long fight to give women the right to vote realized that their involvement in the war might prove that they were worthy of full citizenship. The Scottish Women's Hospitals, supported by the Scottish Federation of Women's Suffrage Societies, were created not only to make a contribution to the war effort or to sidestep the government's blocking their joining the medical military services, but also to prove the basic worth and value of women's abilities. They hoped their efforts would support the belief that women deserved the right to vote.

"Bullets for ballots" was a catchy American anti-suffragette slogan that argued against women receiving the right to vote because they weren't allowed to participate in active military duty. The female doctors associated with the American Women's Hospitals, many of whom were attempting to save the wounded in Europe long before the United States' official involvement, were working, in part, in order to deliberately disprove this slogan.

But women participated in World War I in many other ways: some joined the ranks of fighting men; protestors tried to end their countries' participation in the war; resisters fought against invaders and occupiers of their homelands; other women created and staffed volunteer organizations that attempted to provide support to their countries' troops and relief to war refugees and women and children living in war-devastated areas; and writers

WOMAN'S JOURNAL
AND SUFFRAGE NEWS

VOL. XLIV. NO. 10 — SATURDAY, MARCH 8, 1913 — FIVE CENTS

PARADE STRUGGLES TO VICTORY DESPITE DISGRACEFUL SCENES

Nation Aroused by Open Insults to Women—Cause Wins Popular Sympathy—Congress Orders Investigation—Striking Object Lesson

AMENDMENT WINS IN NEW JERSEY

Easy Victory in Assembly 46 to 5—Equal Suffrage Enthusiasm Runs High

MICHIGAN AGAIN CAMPAIGN STATE

Senate Passes Suffrage Amendment 26 to 5 and Battle Is Now On

General Rosalie Jones in Pilgrim Costume; Miss Inez Milholland on White Steed Leading the Parade; One of the Scores of Imposing Floats; One View of the Procession

Front page of the *Woman's Journal and Suffrage News* describing the hostility experienced by the women who marched for women's suffrage in Washington, DC, on March 3, 1913. *Library of Congress LC-DIG-ppmsca-02970* put themselves in harm's way so that the rest of the world could learn what was really happening.

Most of the women whose stories are included in this book gained fame during or immediately following the war. But these stories don't begin to suggest the enormous number of women who took an active role in the conflict.

Whether these women were doctors or nurses, factory workers or war protestors, soldiers or spies, reporters or relief workers, the way in which they proved themselves in the midst of the carnage and destruction of the First World War is remarkable, especially considering how most men—and even many women—of that time period placed little value on women's abilities outside of the home. Their contributions are a testament to what a determined individual—or group of individuals—can accomplish even in the midst of an otherwise hopeless situation.

BACKGROUND TO WAR

The first official shots of World War I came from Austrian guns on July 29, 1914, when the empire of Austria-Hungary fired across the border into Belgrade, the capital of Serbia. But shots fired one month and one day earlier were the ones that set the war in motion, bullets that ended the life of the man most famously associated with the war: Archduke Franz Ferdinand, heir to the throne of Austria-Hungary.

How and why did this assassination begin a world war? The reasons and their accompanying backstory are complex but can be summarized in a basic notion: the desire for preeminence on the world stage. The major European nations at the time—referred to as the Great Powers—were convinced that a nation was either growing stronger or on the decline, and they were obsessed with belonging to the first group. What was the secret to greatness? One way was to obtain wealth-producing colonies around the world, and the Great Powers were in constant competition with each other to do just that.

Germany, which had only decades before emerged from a loosely connected band of states and become a strong united country, was late to the colony-grabbing game. Often, when seeking new territory, it discovered that Great Britain—arguably the world's greatest power at the time—had gotten there first.

"The [German] people are fed full on the statement that Germany is the nation chosen by Gott [God] to rule the world."

—Josephine Therese, young American
woman in wartime Germany

But German leaders thought it was their nation's time to be the world's major power, and they would not be denied. If they could not compete with Great Britain for colonies, they could compete for the largest navy—one of the reasons for Britain's preeminence. And Germany had become stronger during the 19th century by seizing territory in Europe from France, Denmark, and Austria-Hungary during what were called the German wars of unification. Perhaps the Germans' opportunity for greatness lay not so much in acquiring colonies (although they had some) but in developing military might that could be used to gain more territory in Europe. So in addition to building a series of enormous ships, Germany also began to produce the weapons of war and to enlarge its military in other ways. The other Great Powers—fearing Germany's military buildup while striving to maintain or improve their own greatness—began to do the same as they entered into alliances with other nations, promising assistance in case of war.

"The memory of the Franco-Prussian War of 1870 was still fresh in every heart. We children heard frequent allusions to Alsace and Lorraine; our maps marked the lost provinces in black."

—Louise Thuliez, French resister

Many leaders in each of the Great Powers saw the threat of a new war as an opportunity to gain something for their own countries. For instance, France, still smarting after losing the provinces of Alsace and Lorraine to Germany during the Franco-Prussian War of 1870–1871 (one of the wars of German unification), wanted to get the provinces back. Russia, humiliated after its defeat by Japan during the Russo-Japanese War of 1905, was hoping not only to regain stature among the Great Powers but also to seize land from the Turkish-ruled Ottoman Empire. Great Britain, very content to remain Europe's mightiest power, was uncomfortable with the idea of a German-dominated mainland Europe. Italy, Romania, and Bulgaria, who all came into the war after 1914, did so largely because they had been promised certain territories.

The Austro-Hungarian Empire wanted something too. The many different ethnic groups living there caused constant and significant turmoil within the borders of the mighty but declining empire. Of particular concern were Austria-Hungary's many ethnic Serbians. The bordering nation of Serbia had gained power and land during the Balkan wars of the early 20th century. This led to the notion of creating a Greater Serbia: uniting all Serbians and the lands where they lived into a single nation.

Austria-Hungary had no intention of giving up any of its territory to Serbia and considered the idea of a Greater Serbia to be a direct threat to its sovereignty. So when the ethnic Serbian

Gavrilo Princip shot Franz Ferdinand on June 28, 1914, Austria-Hungary saw the tragic event as a chance to diminish Serbia. Germany agreed to Austria-Hungary's request to support its invasion of Serbia. Russia reacted to Austria's declaration of war against Serbia by mobilizing some of its troops in support of Serbia, its ally. Germany, which shared a border with Russia, responded with its own mobilization.

"I imagine that Austria will not grieve much . . . over the loss of a none too popular crown prince, whose morganatic wife could never be crowned, whose children cannot inherit, and who could only have kept the throne warm for the man who now steps in line a little sooner than he would have had this not happened."

—American journalist Mildred Aldrich on the assassination of Archduke Franz Ferdinand

---

The rest of the previously agreed-upon diplomatic ties went into effect quickly; no country wanted to be in the vulnerable position of being slow to mobilize. So by mid-August, Great Britain, France, and Russia—called the Triple Entente (and later the Allies)—were at war with Germany and Austria-Hungary, referred to as the Central Powers. Men from these nations fought in France and Belgium (referred to as the western front); in Russia, Poland, Austria-Hungary, and Germany (referred to as the eastern front); in the Balkans; and in the Ottoman Empire.

But as the war continued, these were not the only locations where there was fighting, and these nations were not the only ones involved. Before it was over, there would be fighting in the air, at sea, and on land in the Middle East, Africa, Italy, Bulgaria, and Romania by men who came from all over the world, including Canada, Australia, New Zealand, India, Bulgaria, Portugal, Japan, French Indochina, and the United States.

PART I

RESISTERS AND SPIES

"From the day when our King, voicing the mind of his whole people, showed us that our duty lay in resistance to an unjust aggression, I think a burning desire to help in the cause of right possessed us all."

—Princess Marie de Croÿ, Belgian resister

World War I, unlike World War II, did not begin with a clear-cut sense of good versus evil. During World War II, both Germany and Japan were run by governments that were convinced it was their right to take possession of the nations around them and then use—and abuse—the people who lived there.

The motivations that started World War I were similar except that there were not just two nations who felt they had a right to more land. The majority of the nations who became involved in the war did so for just that reason. However, most of them wanted to obtain only certain sections of territory, not entire countries, and in a surprising number of cases, the people living in these areas wanted these border alterations to occur.

Many 19th-century European battles had been fought over borders that constantly shifted with the outcome of each new conflict. This often resulted in people of one ethnic group living on the "wrong" side of a border, separated from others of their ethnicity. These shifting boundaries caused great resentment, both among populations who felt cut off from the rest of their particular nations *and* from governments who had lost land they felt belonged to them, regardless of who lived there.

When World War I was on the horizon, many governments saw it as a way to permanently remedy these situations. But when the conflict began and armies crossed borders, the reactions were vastly different depending on the relationship between the invaded populations and the invaders. For instance, when Romanian soldiers entered Transylvania—part of the Austro-Hungarian empire that was inhabited by many ethnic Romanians—they were welcomed as liberators. However, soldiers entering foreign territory were generally not greeted with similar enthusiasm. And when invasion forces perceived these populations to be hostile, the soldiers sometimes perpetrated abuses. This was especially true when Germany invaded Belgium.

Germany requested permission for its armies to march peacefully through neutral Belgium on their way to Paris. The Belgian government refused and instead sent out its small army to defend its border against the invading Germans.

The Belgian defenses marred the precise timetable that German military commanders had been counting on. Passing quickly through Belgium was the first part of the strategy called the Schlieffen Plan—named after the German officer who had created it years before—that would enable German forces to reach Paris within six weeks. Once there, they had planned to force a French surrender before turning around and focusing their strength on fighting the slow-to-mobilize Russians on Germany's eastern border.

The delay caused by Belgium's armies helped give France—and its ally, Great Britain—a bit of extra time in which to mobilize their troops more effectively. The Germans never reached Paris.

The idea of "Brave Little Belgium"—one of the terms immediately used worldwide to refer to that nation—standing up to one of Europe's largest armies was enough to begin to tip world opinion against Germany. And when reports of the German army's willfully destructive behavior during the invasion began to leak out, Germany's international reputation was ruined. The war suddenly had its good (Belgium) and its evil (Germany).

"The fate that seemed to smile at German audacity now turns against its very arrogance."

—Anna Kuliscioff, Russian-Italian, September 1914

Unmoved by world opinion (and justifying its army's behavior by claiming that Belgian civilians had, against the rules of warfare, fired on them first), the Germans remained in Belgium, occupying all but the far western tip, which they had been unable to take. They also remained in the northeastern section of French territory that they had overrun.

Because they considered the stalemate temporary, the Germans dug trenches on the edges of these occupied territories that would enable them to keep the land they had won and from which they could initiate battles.

"Nothing can describe the feeling of revolt, of nausea almost, that the first sight of the enemy in one's country provokes."

—Princess Marie de Croÿ, Belgian resister

Behind the trenches, the Germans ruled the Belgian and French civilians with an iron fist, killing thousands, sending thousands more into Germany for forced labor, and putting a myriad of occupation laws into place for those who remained. Although the brutality of the German occupation of Belgium and France during the First World War pales in comparison with that of the second, the first German occupation was shocking at the time. Outside of the occupied lands, few people fully understood or even believed the extent of what was happening behind the German trenches on the western front.

But for many of those who were experiencing it, the occupation provoked a determination to fight the Germans in some way: thousands of men and women in occupied nations became involved in some sort of resistance work. Many created and distributed secret underground newspapers designed to combat German propaganda. One such publication, *La Libre Belgique* ("Free Belgium"), was also published during the Second World War.

Many resisters working in Belgium, such as Louise Thuliez and Edith Cavell, were also committed to helping Allied servicemen who had been separated from the rest of their companies, becoming trapped behind enemy lines during the initial battles with the Germans, escape the country. Others, such as Louise de Bettignies and Marthe Cnockaert, worked as spies, gathering information (intelligence) that could be useful to the Allies.

"The English spied on the French and later the Germans; the Italians on the French; the French on the Italians and the Germans; the Russians on the Germans and anyone else they thought necessary. The Germans spied on everyone."

—James Morton, author of *Spies of the First World War* (2010)

In a war where rushing out of the trenches and straight into machine-gun fire was considered ultraheroic, espionage was generally thought to be a shameful but unfortunately necessary wartime activity. Yet during the decades leading up to the war, readers in Great Britain, France, and Germany had become fascinated—and increasingly terrified—by numerous popular novels that featured international spies who were involved with invasion plots geared to bring about a global war. Fact and fiction began to mirror each other as government-sponsored espionage and anti-espionage activities grew increasingly professional throughout Europe, especially in Great Britain and Germany.

The most well-known female spy of World War I was a woman named Mata Hari, but it is doubtful that she provided anyone with any valuable information through her espionage activities.

There were many women, however, who worked very effectively in espionage and anti-espionage activities during the war, both on the home front and behind enemy lines, some for the Central Powers and others for Allied organizations. La Dame Blanche ("The White Lady") was a large and very effective network that gathered information for Great Britain from German-occupied Belgium and France, and it employed women in large numbers, very often in positions of authority.

Mata Hari

The Dutch-born Margaretha Zelle—better known as Mata Hari—is probably the most well-known female spy of World War I (or any time in history), but her lasting fame is for reasons other than the intelligence she gathered. Her exotic dancing costumes, her relationships with many powerful men, and the wild stories that were written about her following her death by firing squad on October 15, 1917—allegedly she exposed herself at the last moment, the firing squad used blanks, she was rescued by one of her many lovers, and so on—all contributed to lasting fame that far exceeded the value of any actual espionage work she may have done. Although the French government executed her for supposedly passing French secrets to Germany, causing the deaths of 50,000 French soldiers, most of the evidence used at her trial was either circumstantial or completely fabricated. While it is clear that Mata Hari took money at

one point from the French government to gather information in Belgium and Spain and on another occasion was referred to by the Germans as spy "H-21," what isn't clear is how important or useful any of her espionage activities were.

Mata Hari in 1910.

Many women who spied for the Central Powers gave their lives in the line of duty. Although the exact total numbers are disputed by historians—they range from 9 all the way to 81—it is clear that many of these women were caught by the French and then shot during the war while others were imprisoned.

World War I had another set of resisters, many who lived in unoccupied countries. These were women who protested their governments' participation in the war. After the initial general enthusiasm began to wane in the face of rising body counts and lowering food supplies, many women throughout the world began war protests. The most dramatic of these protests occurred in Russia on International Women's Day in 1917, when a demonstration of hungry workingwomen in Petrograd became the fuse that helped ignite the Russian Revolution.

But there were a few people—many of them women—who had protested the war from its very beginning. The most famous international gathering of women for the cause of peace during the war took place in the neutral Netherlands for several days in the spring of 1915. This meeting, called the International Congress of Women (also referred to as the Women's Peace Congress) was chaired by American Jane Addams and included more than 1,000 women from many different countries. Some of these women were from combatant countries and had come despite the protests of their governments and, in some cases, their own families. Many of the women who attended the congress resolved to publicly urge world leaders to find a way to end the war, while others returned to lead peace movements in their own countries.

"Shall this war of extermination go on? Women of Europe, where is your voice? The earth reeking of human blood, the millions of wretched bodies and souls of your husbands, sweethearts, and sons. . . . Can these things not rouse you to blazing protest?"

—Lida Gustava Heymann, German war protestor who attended the Women's Peace Congress at The Hague in 1915

The antiwar speaking and writing activities of peace activists often made them very unpopular with their fellow citizens, especially during the initial burst of patriotic enthusiasm at the start of the war. Their views often set them at odds with their own families as well. For instance, British war protestor Charlotte Despard was the sister of top military leader John French. When Charlotte was arrested for her prewar suffragette activities, John said, "I wish she wouldn't do these things, but I can't prevent her." And when the war began, John, then the leader of the British Expeditionary Force in France, was likewise helpless in preventing his older sister from protesting Britain's involvement in the war.

The Pankhursts were another prominent British family dramatically affected by the war. Along with her mother, Emmeline, and her sister Christabel, Sylvia Pankhurst was prominent in the Women's Social and Political Union (WSPU), whose members were the first to be called suffragettes. While Sylvia's concern for the rights of the poor and her questioning of the WSPU's increasingly violent tactics eventually put distance between her and her family—she left their organization in 1913—the war divided them outright. Emmeline and Christabel loudly urged their followers to delay the fight for women's suffrage in order to wholeheartedly support the war effort. In contrast, Sylvia became one of the war's most outspoken critics, attending the Women's Peace Congress at The Hague and helping organize the British Women's Peace Army in 1915 with Charlotte Despard and others.

Not only were war protestors often divided from their families but, when they openly criticized the war, especially as it dragged on year after year, they became dangerously at odds with their governments, who were determined to stay in the conflict. Many protestors in combatant nations were imprisoned.

This type of governmental activity eventually found its way to the United States. Shortly after the United States entered the war in 1917, Congress passed the Espionage Act of 1917 and then the Sedition Act in 1918 (the latter greatly expanded the possibilities for arrest from the Espionage Act). Both laws severely limited free speech related to war protesting. Probably the most famous case involving a violation of the Espionage Act was that of wife, mother, and peace activist Kate Richards O'Hare, who was sentenced to five years in a federal prison (but served less than one) for suggesting in a public speech that "war corrupted motherhood."

Sylvia Pankhurst, social reformer and prominent British war protestor, in 1915.
International Institute of Social History, Amsterdam

EDITH CAVELL

"Patriotism Is Not Enough"

"There are two sides to war—the glory and the misery."

—Edith Cavell, August 1914

On October 7, 1915, German officers crowded into the magnificent Belgian senate chamber in Brussels. The ceiling was decorated with gold. The walls were covered with rich wood paneling. Although the red velvet seats were embroidered with the Lion of Belgium, few Belgians were allowed to attend this event, except those the German officers had come to see. Thirty-five prisoners—most of them Belgian and many of whom had never seen each other before—filed into the room under guard. Six of them were given seats that faced the judges.

Edith Cavell.
St. Mary's Church, Swardeston, Norfolk, United Kingdom

Between each of these six stood a soldier with a fixed bayonet.

The first prisoner called to testify at this trial was not Belgian but British. Her name was Edith Cavell.

The daughter of a vicar, she had been born in Norfolk, England, in 1865. As a young woman, her command of French was so excellent that she was recommended for a governess job in Brussels, Belgium. In 1896, when the children under her charge were grown, she decided to return to London for nurse's training.

In 1907, after working as a nurse for a decade, Edith received a request that was to change her life in ways she could not have imagined. One of Europe's leading surgeons, Dr. Antoine Depage, was seeking to raise the professional standards of Belgian nursing. British nurse training at the time had an excellent reputation, and Dr. Depage was acquainted with the family for whom Edith had worked as a governess. He invited her to become the director of Belgium's first training school for nurses in Brussels.

Edith accepted his offer, and by 1912 her school and clinic, located at 149 rue de la Culture, was providing nurses for three hospitals, three private nursing homes, 24 communal schools, and 13 kindergartens. She was also giving four lectures a week to both doctors and nurses.

Then, in August 1914, Germany invaded Belgium. Great Britain, bound by a treaty made in 1839 to protect Belgian neutrality in case of invasion, declared war on Germany.

The Belgian army was greatly outnumbered by the German one, but many Belgians were still optimistic about victory since Britain had promised to honor their treaty of protection—"We wait for England" was on everyone's lips. But the British troops didn't come as soon as expected. They finally arrived in Belgium around the same time that the Germans entered Brussels, Belgium's capital city.

At 12:40 PM on August 23, 1914, British and German troops clashed for a short time in a small Belgian town called Mons, located 30 miles southwest of Brussels. On August 24, the British Expeditionary Force received orders for a total retreat from Belgium because of superior German numbers and the inability of the French to send reinforcements.

During the retreat many British soldiers were cut off from their regiments and stranded, often because of wounds received during the Battle of Mons. If these soldiers managed to reach a Belgian hospital and were discovered by the Germans, they were ordered out of their beds immediately—no matter their physical condition—and sent to German prison camps.

Warnings against "crimes"—new ones were added daily—were posted on city walls all over Brussels. Hiding Allied soldiers was punishable by death.

Edith responded naturally to authority figures. She ran her own nursing school with fairly strict rules. But her conscience forbade her to obey the German occupiers when it came to turning in Allied soldiers. So when two British men appeared on her doorstep on November 1, 1914, escorted by a Belgian mining official named Herman Capiau, she took them inside without question and hid them for two weeks before plans could be made to take them across the border into the neutral Netherlands.

These two men were the first of many who would pass through her doors. Wounded escapees were given medical care, and those who were healthy were given a hiding place. Then a guide would escort the men across the border into the Netherlands. Edith would often personally escort the men from the clinic to one of six transfer points in Brussels. She would pretend to be merely taking her dog for a walk, using various routes, while the soldiers—disguised as Belgian farmers or miners—followed her from a distance until they made contact with the waiting guide.

Edith also made sure that before leaving the clinic, each soldier had at least 25 francs for the journey. To accomplish this (and also to pay the guides, some of whom wanted money for their efforts), she gave of her own salary and did quiet fundraising as well.

The Germans, always on the lookout for hidden Allied soldiers, would sometimes conduct routine searches at the clinic. On one such occasion, Edith took a British soldier who had just arrived, Lance Corporal J. Doman, put him in a bed, tucking the blankets high above his clothing and fluffing the blankets around the bulge created by his boots, and told the Germans that the "Belgian" in the bed had a serious case of rheumatic fever. The frightened Germans believed her and quickly left the ward. On another occasion, Edith managed to get advance notice of a search just minutes before it happened. She took a wounded British soldier, Charlie Scott, outside and placed him in an apple barrel and covered him with apples. Charlie could hear German boots clicking very close to the apple barrel. But they didn't find him, and several days later Edith hired guides to take him safely to the Dutch border and back to England.

There were many people involved with Edith's resistance network. One of them was Princess Marie de Croÿ, a middle-aged Belgian of noble birth who lived with her brother, Prince Reginald, in a chateau on the Belgian-French border. They began hiding servicemen in their home in October 1914 after being approached by Louise Thuliez (see page 34), a French schoolteacher also determined to help rescue Allied soldiers.

Philippe Baucq, another member of the network, was a Brussels architect heavily involved in distributing copies of *La Libre Belgique* and assisting the escape of Allied soldiers in many ways:

working out escape routes, arranging safe houses for the Allied soldiers, even personally escorting some of them across the border into the Netherlands.

The B branch of the German secret political police, Geheime Politisch Polizei (GPP), was stationed in Brussels and was focused mainly on discovering hidden Allied soldiers and arresting any civilians who were caught helping them. Otto Mayer, a new officer of the Brussels GPP, was specifically assigned to catch Edith Cavell. She was a citizen of Britain, the hated enemy of the Germans, and the GPP strongly suspected she was helping her countrymen escape occupied Belgium, even though the searches of her clinic had so far proved fruitless. Mayer's superior, Lieutenant Bergan, and Bergan's associate Henri Pinkhoff, often repeated the following to each other: *"Die Cavell müss an die Mauer gehen!"* ("The Cavell must go to the wall [before a firing squad]!")

In June 1915, Edith, Herman Capiau, and Louise Thuliez held a meeting. Searches of the clinic by the secret police were becoming more frequent, while the number of men who needed their assistance was growing. Should they continue their work in a limited way, or should they stop altogether? Edith responded this way: "If we are arrested, we shall be punished in any case, whether we have done much or little. So let us go ahead and save as many as possible of these unfortunate men."

Despite Edith's determination to continue, the constant tension was taking its toll on her. Her medical associates noticed that she would suddenly start at unusual noises and would repeatedly pull curtains aside to glance up the street. Later that month, Princess Marie de Croÿ visited Edith in her clinic office. "I wish you hadn't come," Edith said to the princess in a quiet voice. "I am evidently suspect. Look at those men clearing the square in the front," she said. "They have been there several days and are scarcely working at all. They must be set to watch the house." Edith also mentioned that there had been another random search of the clinic on the previous day.

Princess Marie told Edith that her chateau was also under surveillance. She suggested that they cease their work before they were all arrested. Edith at first seemed relieved at this suggestion. But then she asked the princess if there were any men who currently needed help. Yes, the princess replied, Louise Thuliez had just found 30. "Then we cannot stop," said Edith, "because if one of those men got caught and shot it would be our fault."

Suspicious men who were not familiar with the password "yorc" ("Croÿ" spelled backward) began coming to the clinic, asking for help. There were more random searches. Then, on July 31, the German secret police suddenly appeared at the Brussels home of Philippe Baucq and arrested him. Louise Thuliez, who had been staying with the Baucq family for the night, was also arrested. Over the next five days, 35 people involved in the escape network were taken into German custody.

Prince Reginald de Croÿ managed to warn those not yet arrested to go into hiding, including Edith. Edith, who didn't think she'd have a chance of escaping, chose instead to wait for the inevitable while taking the time to destroy any letters or addresses that might incriminate her or anyone else.

On the afternoon of August 5, officers from the German secret police—Pinkhoff and Mayer—arrived at the clinic and, after a thorough search, found a letter from Edith's mother in England that had been transmitted after the occupation of Brussels through the agency of the American Consul. It was not much, but they used it as grounds for arrest. After unleashing a lengthy tirade intended to terrify everyone within hearing, the police took Edith to Saint-Gilles prison, where she was kept in a tiny cell and interrogated on three separate occasions. When she admitted that she had used the clinic to hide healthy Allied soldiers, the Germans realized that Edith was eligible for the death sentence. Under the German penal code, "conducting soldiers to the enemy" was considered treasonous and a capital offense.

Ten weeks later, on October 7, 35 resisters were tried as a group in Belgium's senate chamber. Edith was the first defendant to take the stand. She was asked, "Do you realize that by [helping men escape] it has been to the disadvantage of Germany and to the advantage of the enemy?" Edith replied, "My aim was not to help your enemy but to help those men who asked for my help to reach the frontier. Once across the frontier, they were free."

On October 11, the defendants were marched into a room in the Saint-Gilles prison to hear their sentences read. Some of them were acquitted; some were sentenced to hard labor and others to prison. Five of them heard their names read followed by the German word *Todesstrafe*: the death penalty. One of these was Edith Cavell.

A sympathetic German Lutheran pastor named Paul Le Seur escorted Edith to her cell and was given the task of telling her that she had only hours to live: her sentence was to be carried out the very next day at dawn. He arranged for her to be visited that evening by Rev. Stirling Gahan, an English chaplain whom Edith knew.

When Rev. Gahan arrived in Edith's cell later that evening he was surprised to observe that she was "her bright, gentle, cheerful self, as always, quietly smiling, calm and collected." Edith told him that she valued the 10 weeks she'd been imprisoned—a large part of which she'd spent reading her Bible and *The Imitation of Christ*—because she now realized that it had prepared her to meet death. "Standing as I do in view of God and Eternity," she said to him, "I realize that patriotism is not enough, I must have no hatred or bitterness towards anyone." When it was time to go, Rev. Gahan said, "We shall always remember you as a heroine and a martyr."

"Don't think of me like that," Edith replied. "Think of me only as a nurse who tried to do her duty."

Early in the morning of October 12, 1915, Edith was taken by car to the Belgian national shooting range, the Tir National. Philippe Baucq was to be shot with her. Their sentences were read aloud before a large group of German soldiers. The firing squad of 16 was advised to not hesitate to shoot the woman before them: the nature of her crimes deserved it. Pastor Le Seur was with her right up to the end, and she asked him to relay a message to Rev. Gahan. Speaking in French, she asked that her mother be told that her soul was safe, her conscience at peace, and that *"Je meurs pour Dieu et ma patrie"* (she was dying for God and her country).

Pastor Le Seur then led her to the pole and waited while she was loosely tied and blindfolded. After a brief delay—another pastor was still speaking with Philippe—the firing squad took aim and shot the two people in front of them. Philippe Baucq and Edith Cavell were dead.

When news of Edith's execution hit the presses a few days later, it caused an international outrage. The *New York Times* wrote, "Germany has placed herself in such a situation that the entire world, horror-stricken, will no longer believe that her cause can triumph."

Germany's leader, Kaiser Wilhelm, immediately promised that in the future no woman would be executed without his specific consent. And after being appealed to by several international figures, including the pope, the Kaiser changed the sentences of three remaining condemned prisoners from execution to life in prison.

But his actions came too late to turn the tide on Germany's reputation—the damage had been done. Those involved with British propaganda seized on Edith's execution to stir up hatred of the Germans. Plans to avenge her death included raising an Edith Cavell Machine Gun Regiment and naming battle planes after her, their mission to destroy German cities. And during the weeks immediately following her execution, enlistment numbers in the British army soared.

However, these reactions, which were opposed to Edith's final wish to bear no hatred toward anyone, were temporary. The enthusiasm of young British men to plunge headlong into battle waned as the war dragged on and the death counts soared.

But the story of the brave nurse "who tried to do her duty" and who faced death with calm dignity continued to be a source of inspiration to many long after the guns on the western front fell silent.

A popular postcard offered an erroneous depiction of Edith Cavell's execution, designed to arouse anger toward the Germans. *The Great War Archive, University of Oxford*

LEARN MORE

Edith Cavell
http://edithcavell.org.uk
Includes a full account of Edith Cavell's life and work, with numerous links to other accounts.

Silent in an Evil Time: The Brave War of Edith Cavell by Jack Batten (Tundra Books, 2007).

Edith Cavell by Rowland Ryder (Stein and Day, 1975).

Edith Cavell by Diana Souhami (Quercus, 2010).

LOUISE THULIEZ

"Because I Am a Frenchwoman"

"How mistaken the Germans were if they thought to bring us to heel by force."—Louise Thuliez

On August 2, 1914, schoolteacher Louise Thuliez was in her hometown of Saint-Waast-la-Vallée when the village church bells suddenly began to ring the tocsin—a warning signal. War! French men were immediately mobilized for military action. Most were very eager to fight; they saw it as an opportunity to finally avenge themselves against the Germans who had defeated them in the Franco-Prussian War of 1870–1871. Louise was also eager to do her part. But when she tried to volunteer at several Red Cross hospitals in the area, she was turned away; they already had more than enough nurses.

Louise Thuliez.
Courtesy of Vincent Boez

On the following day, Louise said good-bye to her brother, a priest who was leaving the village to replace a mobilized colleague. He tried to console Louise, who was very discouraged that she hadn't yet found a way to support France in the war. "Don't worry," he said, "God, in His own good time, will give you a chance to serve also."

Troops from Great Britain had come to help the French, but by the end of August they were retreating from the area of Saint-Waast-la-Vallée, overwhelmed by the more numerous invading Germans. Louise listened sadly to the bagpipes that played while the Scottish divisions retreated through the little village. Most of the inhabitants of Saint-Waast-la-Vallée had left too, frightened by the stories they had heard from terrified Belgians who had passed through the village while fleeing the Germans. Out of 800 total villagers, only 60 remained.

Then, on the evening of August 23, 1914, a British regiment, accompanied by several ambulances filled with moderately wounded men, arrived in the village. The regiment was too exhausted to continue on to the nearest Red Cross hospital so the wounded stayed in the village hall for the evening while the rest of the regiment slept on the street. In the morning it turned out that there was no longer room in the ambulances for six of the wounded men. The regiment and their ambulances went on their way, leaving with a promise to return soon with another ambulance to pick up the men. They never came back.

Louise's friend and neighbor Henriette Moriamé brought the six men to her large home while Louise busied herself finding food for them in the deserted village while watching for signs of the impending German invasion. German airplanes flew back and forth over the village while a troop of German cavalry could be seen from a distance on the top of the hill, approaching into the valley village. Finally, at noon, a regiment of Death's Head Hussars—a particular branch of the German cavalry—entered the village in triumph and violence, smashing windows and taking whatever they wanted from the homes and shops, whether or not they were deserted.

When the soldiers saw the British uniforms that the women had washed and spread on the lawn to dry in front of Henriette's home, they demanded entrance. When they discovered the wounded soldiers, they questioned them roughly. But they did little else as they were in a great rush to join the other German soldiers on their way to Paris.

But the German army never made it to Paris: they were stopped at the Marne River by French and British troops. Forced to quickly change their plans, the Germans decided to remain in firm control of the areas they had already taken.

In the autumn, orders were suddenly posted everywhere throughout the German-occupied section of France: all Allied servicemen were to present themselves at the nearest town hall and give themselves up as prisoners. Severe penalties were threatened to all who chose to disobey the order and to any who helped them do so. Louise was determined to help the six men—now healed of their wounds—escape. But she also knew that entire villages were being punished by the Germans for the disobedience of even one person. Therefore the men had to disappear. Near the end of September, Louise and Henriette went to ask Prince Reginald de Croÿ, the owner of a chateau on the border of France and Belgium, if he would help them find shelter for the men. He told them of a cottage in a clearing on the northern border of the large Mormal Forest where another British soldier had already been hiding for two months.

Additional trapped British soldiers joined this group until there were 30 of them. Louise stayed in Obies—a village near the men's hideout—so that she could conveniently keep track of their supplies.

One night there was a report of German patrols nearby. Louise quickly led the men to the de Croÿ chateau, where they arrived at 2:00 AM. Later that morning, the men's captain decided that they should just give themselves up. But Louise and Henriette had already risked so much for the men that they were determined to help them escape. The two women walked 25 miles in the pouring rain to see if they could find some unguarded roads that would lead back to the front lines. When Louise and Henriette returned that evening with the knowledge of some possible routes, the men refused to listen. While the women had been gone, the soldiers had decided that it wasn't honorable to continue to allow women to put themselves in so much danger for them.

Louise and Henriette helped the men travel to Bavay, where the men planned to turn themselves in to the Germans. Louise and Henriette returned to their village discouraged. They later learned that the men hadn't revealed anything when questioned about how they had managed to survive in the woods but that the Germans decided that the villagers of Bavay must have helped them. So the villagers were punished with a heavy fine, and their mayor was taken hostage. The British men were sent to a prison camp in Wittenberg where they remained for the rest of the war.

Then one day in December 1914, Louise received some good news: a method to help British and other Allied servicemen to escape from German-occupied France had been discovered. The journey's destination was the neutral country of the Netherlands, and the main stopping point was the German-occupied city of Brussels in Belgium. After traveling to Brussels to see for herself if the route would work, Louise came back to the chateau and within two hours was headed back with two British officers and Prince Reginald de Croÿ. Louise and Prince Reginald escorted the officers to a safe house in Brussels, where they left them, knowing that their safe passage into the Netherlands had already been arranged.

Now that they had found a workable route, Louise and Henriette busied themselves with finding more Allied soldiers. Although the battles of Charleroi and Mons, which had stranded many British soldiers, had occurred near the beginning of the war, many French villagers had risked hiding them all these months.

Each rescue operation was slightly different but Louise and Henriette eventually established a somewhat regular routine. The first step was to gain the trust of the French villagers. This was not always easy. Once some villagers, convinced the women were responsible for the arrest of some hidden British soldiers, dug two graves for them, determined to kill them when they saw them next. Only the local priest, who firmly believed the women were on the side of the Allies, prevented this from happening.

But once trust was gained and the soldiers turned over to their care, Louise and Henriette would make their way to the de Croÿ chateau, usually by passing through the forest of Mormal. Getting into the forest from certain areas sometimes proved to be challenging; Henriette and Louise often had to be very creative in finding their way inside. While ferrying hidden soldiers from a certain area called Maroilles they found that the only way to enter the forest was by crossing a heavily guarded railway line. They decided to overcome this obstacle by disguising the soldiers as French woodcutters who were traveling to the forest for firewood. The disguised soldiers would mutter a *bonjour* as they waited for the Germans to open the railway gate that would allow them access to the forest. They would then wait in the forest until dark before heading for the de Croÿ chateau. After the women rescued several groups in this way, they were told that the Germans at the railway gate were becoming curious about why so many woodcutters entered the forest but never returned.

Louise and Henriette not only had to convince suspicious villagers that they were working for the Allies, they sometimes had to convince the soldiers as well. They once made arrangements with some villagers to escort two soldiers, an Englishman and a Canadian, to safety. The soldiers failed to appear at the scheduled time and place. Instead, the Canadian left a letter for the women saying that he did not trust them. But after wandering the countryside for a few weeks they suddenly reappeared with some other trapped soldiers and said they were now ready to follow. After Louise escorted them to Brussels and returned, she became puzzled at how the villagers expressed visible relief upon her return. They explained, "We could not warn you beforehand but the Canadian had loaded his revolver before leaving, declaring that if they had the slightest difficulty en route the bullet was for you."

When they reached the de Croÿ chateau, the escaping soldiers would receive false identity cards before continuing on, usually the following day. Once they set out, they took lengthy detours and unfrequented roads. Passing motorists, German service wagons, and German foot patrols on the road also slowed things down, but the women devised a system to avoid being caught: either Louise or Henriette would walk ahead of the rest of the party, and if there was danger, the woman in front would drop a white handkerchief as a signal to the rest of the party to take cover.

After crossing the French-Belgian border Louise and Henriette would leave the men at a safe house within a little Belgian village; someone else would escort the men to Brussels from there.

In February 1915, Louise met Herman Capiau, who in turn introduced her to Edith Cavell. They all began to work together. Louise would take the Allied soldiers she located in France to the Belgian border, and then Herman would take them to Edith's clinic in Brussels. From there they would eventually find safe passage across the Dutch border. After a while, Louise herself began escorting men found in northern France all the way to Brussels, personally leaving them with Edith. When the clinic became too crowded, Louise found other hiding places for the men.

On the night of July 31, 1915, Louise was in Brussels at the home of Philippe Baucq, a Belgian architect heavily involved in resistance with whom Louise had begun working a few months earlier. She had been staying in the city, but as they had much to discuss, Philippe invited her to stay the night with his family. She called at the Baucq household at 10:45 PM. The whole family—including two girls, ages 11 and 14—was busy folding freshly printed copies of the illegal underground newspaper *La Libre Belgique*.

At about 11:30, Mrs. Baucq showed Louise to her upstairs room. Meanwhile, Philippe opened the door to let his dog out. Louise suddenly heard it barking furiously. A group of men was shouting. It was the Germans!

They barged in, ran upstairs, and demanded to see the woman they had just seen enter the house. Louise ran into the bathroom and tried to hide her handbag, but they chased and questioned her. What was her name? She gave them her most recent alias: Madame LeJeune.

"Where then," they asked, "is your husband?"

She paused for a moment and then said that they were separated. They asked for her address. She couldn't give away the addresses of any of the safe houses where she regularly stayed, so she said that she had no fixed address. Her vague answers made the soldiers very suspicious, so they locked her in one of the rooms as they searched the rest of the house. They found thousands of copies of *La Libre Belgique* and several other illegal pro-Belgian publications, plus various lists of addresses (some relating to illegal newspaper subscribers) and visiting cards (cards visitors left with their names and other information). The Germans took Louise and Philippe to the jail at Saint-Gilles. When Sergeant Henri Pinkhoff, the German officer in charge of their arrest, arrived with them at the prison he said to the other Germans there, *"Endlich, endlich"* ("At last, at last").

Louise, Philippe, Edith, and many others were all brought to trial on the same day, October 7, 1915. Louise was called to the stand directly after Edith. She was asked many questions designed to reveal the organizational system of the escape network; the Germans wanted to know who was in charge. But they were disappointed: this group had worked together on terms of equality. There was no "chief."

When they had finished questioning Louise and she was in the process of returning to her seat, the prosecutor suddenly asked her one more question: What had been her motive for becoming involved in rescuing Allied soldiers? "Because I am a Frenchwoman," she replied.

All of the court proceedings were conducted in German, with French translators for the prisoners. When they heard their sentences read on October 11, the prisoners heard one German word repeated five times: *"Todesstrafe."* When the interpreter read the sentences in French, they realized what *Todesstrafe* meant: five of them, including Philippe, Edith, and Louise, had been sentenced to death.

Louise woke up at six the following morning with a feeling of dread. "I am afraid," she said to her cellmate, "afraid for Edith

Cavell." She later found out that Edith had been executed earlier that morning.

But Louise's life was to be spared. The German kaiser, embarrassed by the international outrage caused by Edith's execution, quickly had the death sentences of the remaining condemned prisoners of the group commuted to life in prison. Transferred temporarily to the Cambrai prison, Louise requested a china bowl to replace the filthy tin one that contained her water. Her request was refused on the grounds that broken china might be used for a suicide attempt. Louise replied that she was "far too proud of being in prison for my country" to attempt suicide.

In January 1916, Louise was transferred to the prison in Siegburg, Germany, where she was released by mutinying male prisoners a few days before the armistice in November 1918. She returned to her hometown to find it devastated and her own home looted.

After the war she handed French statesman Georges Clemenceau a list of women she thought should be officially recognized for their resistance work. After he looked at the list, he said to Louise, "You have forgotten one person on this list."

When Louise protested, Clemenceau told her that she should have included herself. He awarded her with the Croix de Guerre and the Legion of Honor.

After the war Louise worked on behalf of French female suffrage and published her memoir, *Condemned to Death*, in 1933.

During World War II, while in her late 50s, Louise worked with another escape line and afterward received an additional Military Cross from France.

She died in Paris on October 10, 1966.

LEARN MORE

Condemned to Death by Louise Thuliez (Methuen and Company, 1934) translated from the French by Marie Poett-Velitchko.

"Condemned with Edith Cavell: Story of Louise Thuliez, Belgian School Teacher Who Was Saved from Death by the King of Spain, Now Told by Herself," *New York Times*, May 11, 1919. Download a PDF of the original article at http://query.nytimes.com/gst/abstract.html?res=F2071EFC3D5E157A93C3A8178ED85F4D8185F9

War Memories by Princess Marie de Croÿ (Macmillan and Company, 1932).

EMILIENNE MOREAU

The Teen Who Became
a National Symbol

It was October 1915. Neither the Germans nor the British and French had gained a significant advantage over the other on the western front. Military leaders on both sides of the gridlock tried to create *the* plan, a "Big Push" that would lead to a decisive victory and end the war.

None of these leaders realized that a teenage girl would be forever associated with a battle that would emerge from one of these plans. The name of that girl was Emilienne Moreau.

Emilienne had been 16 years old when the Germans invaded France in August 1914. She had been studying that summer for her teacher's certification. Her father, Henri, a recently retired

Emilienne Moreau.
Musée de l'ordre de la libération

coal mining foreman who had raised his family in a series of mining camps, had recently moved his family to Loos, a mining town of 4,000 people, where he had opened a small grocery store.

Emilienne's brother, named Henri after his father, had joined the armed forces the moment the war had begun, like most of the other young men in Loos. Those who remained behind—women, children, and older men—tried to make sense of the conflicting rumors they heard regarding the clash of armies far away. The French press, like the presses in the other combatant countries, was heavily censored and light on facts; it only emphasized the courage of the French soldiers and the effectiveness of their weapons.

When streams of Belgian refugees began to pass through Loos, however, everyone knew that things could not possibly be going well for the French and their British allies. Many residents fled Loos at this point, but the Moreaus decided to stay. They were one of the few families still left when the Germans appeared, trashed the entire town, and looted the Moreaus' store. The soldiers then installed machine guns on top of the mine pit towers (approximately 72 feet high) to defend the area from the French and British, should they attempt to follow.

And follow they did. Shortly after the Germans arrived, Emilienne was looking out the window of her attic when she saw French troops walking in the direction of the machine gun nests. In spite of the danger, Emilienne ran out of her house and warned one of the leaders to stop—he was leading his troops to their deaths. Though surprised, the leader listened to her advice. And just in time. The Germans fired on the French soldiers as they ran for cover behind a church wall. The French remained for a few days of house-to-house fighting, but after being overwhelmed by the Germans, they left Loos quietly, beginning on the night of October 10.

The Germans were now in complete control of the village, and they let the inhabitants know it. They conducted random and constant searches, warning the people of Loos that they would be severely punished if they were caught hiding any Allied soldiers. Food became scarce as the Germans rationed everything that they hadn't taken for themselves. In order to survive, the Moreaus created an unappealing but edible bread substitute made from wheat grains ground in a coffee mill.

The Germans also established a strict curfew. One evening in November, Emilienne's father stayed outside too late. He was arrested, accused of being a spy, and narrowly escaped being shot by a firing squad. Emilienne pleaded for her father's freedom until at last the Germans let him go.

But the older man had been traumatized by his experience in German custody. He refused to leave the house, hiding in the attic all day and night. After one month of suffering from his fears and exhausted by the lack of food, Henri Moreau died. Emilienne and the rest of her family made a coffin on their own, using some planks that had been left by the town carpenter.

After her father's funeral, Emilienne noticed Loos children playing in the rubble every day, obviously not attending school—without teachers and with few children remaining in the town, the schools were closed. She began to teach some of them in one of the village's abandoned homes. Because there was so little fuel to keep them warm, Emilienne and her students would regularly visit the slag heaps of coal pit number 15. During each trip, while collecting remnants of coal, Emilienne would make a mental note of German defenses—such as nests of machine guns—on the coal pit. She realized that if the French ever returned, this area might become an area of intense fighting.

She was right. In September of the following year, the French asked the British to support an attack on the Germans—it would be referred to as the Loos-Artois Offensive, part of the larger Champagne-Artois Offensive. The attack would involve moving British soldiers into Loos to recapture the area from the Germans. Then the British planned to continue south where they thought they could surround the Germans. Approximately 100,000 British troops were sent into Loos and the surrounding areas.

On September 25, 1915, the battle of Loos began. The roof of the Moreau home had been destroyed by Allied artillery a few

Poisoned Gas and the Battle of Loos

The Battle of Loos was the first time British troops attempted to use poison gas against the Germans on the western front (the Germans had used it first on the Allies at the second Battle of Ypres in April 1915). For this battle, British general Douglas Haig ordered 5,000 six-foot-long cylinders of chlorine, each of them weighing 150 pounds, to be carried through the trenches to the front lines of battle. But the gas released by the British on the first day of the Battle of Loos didn't have the effect they had hoped for. The wind was slow, and by the time some of the chlorine gas reached the German lines, the soldiers were wearing their gas masks. Some of the gas blew into no-man's-land (the section of territory between the trenches), where it stayed, while in other areas the wind sent it back into the British trenches.

While both sides worked hard to improve the quality of their gas masks, poison gas continued to be used—with deadly results—for the duration of the war.

La Guerre 1914-15-16
Visé Paris

LOOS (P.-de-C.) - Les ruines de l'Église de Loos.

Edition Deschamps - Béthune

The church in Loos after the battle. *Courtesy of Paul Reed*

days earlier. But instead of finding a safe shelter during the battle, Emilienne ascended the attic stairs of her family's roofless home to get a view of the situation to see if she could find a way to help. A strange yellow cloud kept her from seeing clearly, but when she heard gunfire coming from the cemetery, she knew that the Allies were heading toward several deadly nests of German machine guns just outside of Loos.

Emilienne ran down the stairs, out of the house, and toward the tombs. She saw what looked like "strange beings with enormous eyes," who seemed to have pipes for noses. And to top it all off, these strange creatures were wearing skirts. They were Scottish soldiers wearing kilts and gas masks: the Highlanders of the Ninth Black Watch, so named because their kilts were dark.

Emilienne, who didn't speak English, frantically tried to make one of the officers understand that his men were walking toward their deaths. She offered to guide them in such a way that they would avoid the gun nests in the tower bridge and the long slag heap.

With Emilienne's help the Scottish troops moved safely around the gun nests and took them out. Then they went on past Loos to destroy a fortified German position. But because they had moved faster than the regiments to their left, they were forced to retreat back to Loos, which they were determined to keep from the Germans. The Germans were equally determined to return. That afternoon an intense house-to-house battle between the Scots and the Germans erupted in the midst of the village.

The Moreau home was quickly transformed into a makeshift rescue and first-aid station. The doctor in charge taught Emilienne how to clean and bandage wounds. She sometimes also helped severely wounded Scottish soldiers reach the rescue station.

On the following day Emilienne saw some German soldiers enter the cellar of the house that was directly opposite the Moreau house. Then she saw them take aim through the bars of the cellar window. Their target? A visibly wounded Scottish soldier who was struggling toward the Moreau rescue station.

Enraged, Emilienne grabbed a sack of grenades lying nearby, which had been left by one of the wounded men in the station. Assisted by three wounded soldiers who could walk, she threw some of the grenades directly down the stairs of the cellar of the opposite house. The explosion killed the Germans.

The Moreau house was not large, and the Scottish and British wounded kept coming. The rescue station was expanded to include the house next door. An enormous hole was made in one of the walls so that the seriously wounded men—stretcher cases—could be moved in and out more easily.

Shortly after that, Emilienne was caring for a wounded British soldier in the expanded station when a bullet suddenly whizzed through a hole in the wall and just past her head. When she turned to see where the bullet had come from, she saw the silhouettes of two approaching Germans. She grabbed a revolver that had been left by one of the male nurses and fired, killing both Germans. Trembling because she had never fired a gun before, she called out for help. An officer came over and congratulated her, shaking her hand.

On the following day a German shell hit the Moreau home. Emilienne's sister was badly wounded in her arm. Because she needed serious medical attention, because the fighting was becoming increasingly intense, and because the Scottish troops were now requesting that the civilians move out of the area, Emilienne, her sister, and their mother all traveled to the hospital in the town of Béthune—first on foot, then by cart, and finally, in an army truck.

When they reached the hospital they were grieved to learn that Emilienne's brother, Henri, had been killed several months earlier. They also met someone they hadn't seen in a while: the doctor who had been working with Emilienne at Loos. He was now working at this same hospital and told everyone what Emilienne had done to save the Scottish patients.

Emilienne began to receive a series of awards and medals from key people in the British military and government, including King George: she had suddenly become a living symbol of the French-British alliance. But she had also become a symbol of hope for the French, who were overwhelmed by the enormous number of French soldiers who had been killed by this point. When the French newspapers published photographs of Emilienne winning the Military Cross while dressed in black (in mourning for her brother), it was as if she were suddenly

Newspaper photo of Emilienne (center) and others receiving the French
Military Cross. *Musée de l'ordre de la libération*

representing all the women of France: grieving yet undefeated.

When German military leaders heard the story, however,
they threatened to shoot on the spot every armed French civilian that they encountered. Emilienne's actions confirmed their
suspicion that the French government was regularly arming its
citizens in violation of the international rules of warfare.

The French and British press ignored the German threats,
countering that Emilienne had been justified in shooting the
Germans since they were trying to kill the wounded, something that was also illegal according to international law.

The French government and press saw Emilienne's story as
a powerful tool with which to strengthen and continue civilian
support of the war. She was paid to write her memoir by *Le Petit
Parisien*, a newspaper with an enormous circulation. Her photo-
graph began to appear everywhere—from the soldier's quarters
to public subways—with descriptions that compared her to Joan
of Arc.

Her popularity endured throughout the war and afterward, but by the late 1930s it suddenly went into sharp decline. The French didn't want to offend the Germans—whose military might was once again casting an enormous shadow over Europe—by reminding them that a French heroine had become so by killing German soldiers. Adolf Hitler reportedly said that he "would have dispatched two members of the Nazi Party to assassinate her!"

Emilienne managed to stay out of Hitler's way when German troops occupied France during World War II. However, she didn't work very hard to stay out of harm's way altogether: she became actively involved in the Resistance movement through the Brutus Network, carrying messages under her clothes—wedged in with bandages and padding—while pretending to be pregnant. She was often tracked by the Gestapo but was able to elude their grasp by constantly changing her appearance.

Following the Second World War, Emilienne was once again honored by the French government and was elected to the French National Assembly, where she worked for decades to promote women's rights. Although her memoir was out of print by the time of her death in 1971, several streets and schools are named after her in the northernmost areas of France.

LEARN MORE

The Battle of Loos by Philip Warner (William Kimber, 1976).

GABRIELLE PETIT

Feisty Patriot

It was 1911 in Brussels, Belgium. Nineteen-year-old Gabrielle Petit had just survived an attempted suicide. She had discovered that the man with whom she had been making wedding plans was already married and the father of several children.

Gabrielle had been troubled long before she met her married beau. Her father had never seemed to love her or any of his family. Obsessed with becoming a great inventor and with his distant relation to a noble line, Jules Petit behaved as if the jobs necessary to support his family were beneath his dignity. He wasted his money and fell deeply into debt. So destitute that they were forced to sell their furniture, Gabrielle's parents fought constantly.

Gabrielle Petit.
Author's collection

When Gabrielle's mother, to whom she had been close, died at the age of 33, nine-year-old Gabrielle wound up at an orphanage and boarding school run by nuns (her older sister had been sent to a different school earlier). The nuns found Gabrielle very difficult to manage: she was often quarrelsome and seldom conformed to the rules. Her mother had been able to manage her sometimes difficult personality because of their loving relationship, but given the limited resources and staffing of the orphanage, personal attention there was nearly impossible. So while Gabrielle flourished academically, she also felt emotionally abandoned and resentful.

While Gabrielle was away at school her father married a much younger woman. Although Gabrielle didn't see him often, their relationship wasn't entirely negative. In fact, one day he sent her a box of candy. Unfortunately, this was against school rules. One of the other parents, when she learned of Gabrielle's gift, wrote a letter of complaint to Jules Petit, who in turn wrote an angry response letter to the mother superior. Gabrielle was soon in trouble, not only for having the candy but also for allegedly complaining to her father (although she hadn't). She was told she must either submit to punishment or leave. Only 15 years old, Gabrielle chose to leave the school rather than receive an unfair punishment. She went to live with her father and his new wife.

Quickly realizing that the new living situation would never work and feeling rejected again by her father, Gabrielle began a life of constant upheaval. Because she didn't take criticism well, she moved from job to job. She tried to get into a public school to train to be a teacher but was turned down. Dejected, she embarked on a period of wild living that culminated in the attempt on her own life.

But then a couple named Collet-Sauvage, who lived in the same building as Gabrielle, took her into their home and cared for her. In doing so, they provided her with the first true happiness she had known since before her mother had died. Gabrielle became happy and radiant. Although the only work she could find was as a waitress in a tavern—for which the late hours required that she live in the same building—she knew now that she would always have an adopted home with the Collet-Sauvages.

One day early in 1914, a young man named Maurice Gobert, a sergeant in the light infantry who was seated with his friends at the tavern, saw her and asked if he could start dating her. Gabrielle soon fell deeply in love with him and made enormous life changes. She returned to church and got a different job, away from the tavern, and they became engaged. Gabrielle was convinced that she was on her way to lasting happiness.

But that happiness was suddenly interrupted when, on August 3, 1914, Maurice had to join his regiment as the whole Belgian army followed the king's orders to defend Belgium against the invading Germans. Gabrielle wanted to volunteer to work as a nurse in the infirmary serving Maurice's regiment but could not, so instead she joined the Red Cross in Brussels, working as a first-aid volunteer.

During her spare time, Gabrielle collected funds for the soldiers door-to-door as well as from passersby in public places. "Considering I have a lot of nerve," she wrote Maurice, "I do a very good business." But no matter how much money she collected on behalf of the Belgian army, Gabrielle couldn't do anything to change the strength and size of the German one.

On August 20, the Germans entered Brussels. Wave after wave of uniformed Germans marched through the city, singing "Die Wacht am Rhein," the militaristic unofficial German national anthem. They shut down the Red Cross. Gabrielle soon learned that a week earlier Mr. Collet-Sauvage had died during the invasion. Then she received news that Maurice had been seriously wounded. It seemed that the Germans were in the process of destroying the only true happiness Gabrielle had ever known.

She left Brussels to stay with her future parents-in-law near Charleroi, south of Brussels. Maurice was able to escape from the hospital in Antwerp as the Germans began to surround it, and he found his way home to Charleroi.

The Germans—on the lookout for Belgian soldiers—got word that Maurice was in his parents' home, forcing him to go into hiding in a nearby town. Gabrielle also left the Gobert home to try to locate Mrs. Collet-Sauvage.

During the couple's separation, Maurice's parents tried to convince him to break his engagement with Gabrielle, whom they didn't like at all. In fact, some "helpful friend" in communication with Maurice's father met him in Belgium and recounted tales of Gabrielle's supposedly wild living in Maurice's absence. (They were actually descriptions of the life she had lived before meeting the Collet-Sauvages.) When Gabrielle and Maurice were reunited in Brussels in May 1915, she was able to dispel the false rumors and convince him of her sincere love for him.

But things continued to unravel. Someone had betrayed Maurice's parents and three friends to the Germans for hiding him. Maurice's sister, Nelly, who also disliked Gabrielle and was determined to separate the couple, told Maurice that Gabrielle had been the betrayer. It also seems likely that Nelly gave Gabrielle's address to the Germans, for she too was soon arrested. During her arrest, the Germans found many letters addressed to Maurice. When presented to the Goberts, this created the impression that Gabrielle had given these documents to the Germans as part of a betrayal. Not knowing of Gabrielle's arrest, Maurice wrote his sister that he was done with Gabrielle.

Shortly afterward he was able to escape occupied Belgium and rejoin what was left of his regiment in France.

Gabrielle, released from German custody after only 48 hours and not realizing that Maurice had broken their engagement, was now obsessed with rejoining him in France. She took the standard route to escape the German occupation: traveling on foot to the Netherlands, by boat to England, and from there to unoccupied France.

On the ship to England, Gabrielle began talking with a British officer, expressing her desire to volunteer for medical work in France. The soldier was struck by her bold personality and passionate commitment to the Allied cause. He asked if she would be willing to work as an agent in Belgium for British intelligence.

She was ecstatic and wrote to Maurice that instead of working near him, she was going to start a different sort of work, the details of which needed to be kept secret but that she knew he would approve of. It would necessarily keep them apart but, she wrote, "We will be separated for a common cause." Gabrielle was thrilled that British intelligence was going to give her money; not only could she repay those who had been kind to her but she and Maurice would have enough to live on when they were married.

Gabrielle didn't receive a response to this or to any of her letters to Maurice, but she thought that the war was somehow preventing him from writing her back. She never dreamed that he had broken with her.

On August 2, 1915, after training in England, Gabrielle was ready. Her alias was to be "Miss Legrand." Her "letter box"—the person to whom she would drop off her collected information—was Mrs. Collet-Sauvage. Gabrielle would be responsible for reporting the size, location, type, and movements of enemy troops, trains, and munitions along with road conditions and bridge widths, primarily in the area of her native city of Tournai, in south central Belgium. She also distributed copies of the illegal underground newspaper *La Libre Belgique* and assisted Belgians who were trying to leave the country.

Traveling from place to place, Gabrielle often changed her appearance in order to collect information. Her previous frequent job changes now served her well as she disguised herself as a door-to-door hat saleswoman, a newspaper seller, a beggar, a fisherman, a nanny, a barmaid, and a bakery delivery woman.

She took notes regarding her observations on very thin paper with corrosive invisible ink, which she delivered to her letter box, Mrs. Collet-Sauvage. Special couriers would then visit Mrs. Collet-Sauvage periodically and make sure that the British got the information.

Gabrielle had found her calling, apparently what she had been born to do. "At no time was I happier," she wrote to members of her family. Not only did she love the sense of adventure she received from her activities but working as an agent had filled her with a new patriotism. "My country!" she wrote in a letter, "I did not think enough of it, I almost ignored it. I did not see that I loved her. But since they torment her, the monsters, I see her everywhere. I breathe her in the streets of the city, in the shadow of our palace . . . she lives in me, I live in her. I will die for her singing." Where in the past she was constantly worn out just trying to survive, she now had the energy to help others: she found time to care for a sick friend, assemble care packages for soldiers at the front, and generously reimburse those who were working with her.

German counterespionage agents knew someone was successfully operating in Gabrielle's area. As she had a reputation of openly ridiculing the German occupiers, she attracted their notice. Early in 1916, they set a clever trap for Gabrielle, and her connection to British intelligence was made clear (although her specific work was not). While staying with Mrs. Collet-Sauvage, she was arrested.

As she was driven away in the Germans' car, Gabrielle shouted out the window to all passersby, "I am Belgian and I am captive of Boches!" One of the soldiers in the car threatened her with violence. "Just try it," she replied. "I will pierce your hand with the hairpin of my hat!" While in prison, she made as much noise as possible—shouting, banging on the heating pipes, and singing the Belgian national anthem and another patriotic Belgian march as loudly as possible while covering the walls of her cell with anti-German graffiti.

Her trial was held in the Belgian senate chamber, where she peppered the proceedings with loud protestations against the blatantly unjust trial. She refused to answer any questions but freely admitted to working in espionage and said that she would continue doing so if set free. "I do not fear you," she said. "Kill me. I will only be replaced. The work will go on. That is what gives me pleasure!"

The Germans hadn't actually found much concrete evidence of her particular involvement in espionage, but during the trial she gave them all the information they needed to condemn her to death. Somebody tried to get her to plead with the kaiser for her life, but she refused, explaining to the prison vicar, "I will not abase myself before a German, even less before the kaiser. I want to show them how a Belgian woman knows how to die."

The German governor of Belgium, hesitating to execute another woman after the international outrage that had followed Edith Cavell's execution months before in October 1915, sent the decision to the kaiser in Berlin. Gabrielle, never knowing which day would be her last, remained amazingly calm throughout her time in prison, as witnessed (and admired) by her German translator and all who came into contact with her.

The kaiser rejected a clemency plea from Gabrielle's family: she would receive the death penalty. She spent her last night writing good-bye letters to family and friends, including Maurice, who she believed was still her fiancé. Unbeknownst to Gabrielle, Maurice had already married another woman.

On April 1, 1916, Gabrielle was led to the Tir National shooting range, where she refused to be blindfolded. Just before the soldiers fired, Gabrielle cried out, *"Vive la Belgique! Vive—!"* ("Long live Belgium!") before the guns silenced her voice and took her life.

Gabrielle was not the only woman to give her life for her country during the Belgian occupation, but she became one of the most famous, due more to her feisty personality and the eloquent confidence shown at her trial than for any information she had provided the British. Her passionate love for Belgium was seen as the embodiment of the Belgian resistance.

In 1919 Gabrielle's body was exhumed and reburied in a state funeral. In the years immediately following, statues were erected in her honor, while books, plays, songs, and films were dedicated to her memory. Belgium, a relatively new country composed of Flemish (Germanic) and Walloon (French) components, was united in its admiration for Gabrielle. And in the 1930s, when the Nazis began to make it clear that Germany was again preparing for war, Belgian veterans of World War I began to invoke the memory of Gabrielle's resistance as they sought to prepare Belgians for the inevitable.

When the Germans occupied Belgium once more during World War II, they found evidence that the memory of Gabrielle Petit was inspiring more enthusiasm for resistance than they cared to deal with: so many flowers began appearing at the foot of one of her statues that guards were posted there to prevent further tributes to the feisty girl who had loved her country and given her life on its behalf.

LEARN MORE

"Gabrielle Petit"
Public Radio Exchange (PRX)
www.prx.org/pieces/93162-gabrielle-petit
From the "In Your Face Women" series, KSLU (PRX Radio).

MARTHE CNOCKAERT

Nurse for the Germans, Spy for the Belgians

"Because I am a woman and I could not serve my country as a soldier I took the only course open to me."

—Marthe Cnockaert

"The Germans have invaded Belgium!" It was the evening of August 4, 1914, and Marthe Cnockaert's father had just rushed into the kitchen of their Westrozebeke farmhouse to tell his wife and daughter the terrible news. "King Albert has ordered general mobilization." Marthe went out to tell her brothers they would now be part of the Belgian armed forces.

Marthe Cnockaert in 1914.
I Was a Spy! (1934)

When the German army reached Westrozebeke, a young German officer falsely accused Marthe's father of being a sharp-shooter and tried to burn him alive in his own house. Although her father was able to escape through the back of the burning house while the Germans stood watch in front, Marthe and her family were now homeless. After they were taken in by a neighbor, Marthe—who had received some medical training prior to the war—volunteered to alleviate the suffering of the soldiers, both German and Allied, who were filling the emergency hospital set up across the street.

In January 1915, Marthe and her mother moved to Rousselaere (today spelled Roeselare), a Belgian town very close to the fighting, where Marthe again found work as a nurse at a hospital. Two weeks after their arrival Lucelle Deldonck, a middle-aged family friend from Westrozebeke, walked into the house where Marthe and her mother had found shelter. She looked

Francs-Tireurs and the Invasion of Belgium

The Germans were extremely harsh toward civilians who fired on German troops. These civilians were referred to in French as *francs-tireurs* ("free shooters"). Initially the Great War was considered a civilized conflict fought by professional, trained soldiers. So, to the German way of thinking, these armed civilians were threatening the social order when they fired on the soldiers invading their homeland. More than 1,000 Belgian civilians were killed during the initial phase of the war in retaliation for supposed attacks on the German army.

exhausted. She told them that she had just crossed over the border between Belgium and the neutral Netherlands, and she had good news: Marthe's three brothers were safe. About to leave, Lucelle suddenly turned back and asked, "Marthe, would you like to serve your country?

Somehow Marthe knew immediately that Lucelle was asking her to become a spy. She was filled with a sense of horror. She knew that there were spies in Belgium working for the Allies, but she had no desire to become one. Espionage had the reputation of being a sneaky, underhanded profession. But her mother spoke first: "If my daughter wishes to serve I give her willingly and proudly, just as I have given my sons."

After another moment's hesitation, Marthe agreed. Lucelle then told her that she was actually working for British Intelligence and that someone would soon contact Marthe about her possible work.

Three days later, an old woman the Germans called Canteen Ma, who sold vegetables from house to house in her horse-drawn cart, greeted Marthe as she left her house for her work at the hospital. The old woman tried to interest Marthe in some beans, but just as Marthe was about to call the house servant, the old woman slipped a tiny piece of folded paper into Marthe's hands. It contained directions for a meeting with someone named Lisette. When Marthe arrived at the destination, she found that Lisette was a code name for her friend Lucelle.

Lucelle told Marthe to keep her ears open while working at the Rousselaere hospital. Because Rousselaere was so near the fighting, Marthe was in a strategic position to overhear important snippets of conversation from the Germans regarding troop movements, the locations of ammunition dumps, and more. After giving her a few more particulars and alerting her to the impending visit of a so-called safety pin man—a Belgian resister who would identify himself by revealing two safety pins hidden under his collar—Lucelle gave Marthe one last warning: "A spy needs above all else to keep her wits about her every moment of her life, asleep or awake—eyes, ears, brains and intelligence are the tools of a good spy." Then she added, "If you are caught it will in all probability be your own fault."

Two days later, a safety pin man came to the house and gave Marthe her first assignment. She took the message he'd given her to a window in an alleyway that had been specified by Lucelle. She tapped on the window three times, waited, and then tapped twice more. A hand, white against the darkness, lifted the window, silently took the note from Marthe, and disappeared again. Marthe had successfully made contact with "Number 63."

After working between Canteen Ma and Number 63 to send many reports this way and helping several wounded Allied prisoners escape from the hospital, Marthe was given a new opportunity in March 1915. Her father—who had been able to join his family after his brush with death—had become the owner of a café in Rousselaere where many German servicemen spent their free time. Marthe decided that working evenings in the cafe might give her access to additional information. One day Marthe found that three Germans had decided to take rooms in the apartments above the café. One of them, especially, seemed very pleasant, and Marthe couldn't help but like him. But her opinion of him changed when she got a surprise visit from some safety pin men. They warned Marthe that the very German she found so pleasant—Otto von Promft—had been sent to the café specifically to weed out spies among the local Belgians.

One day Marthe was summoned into the office of the hospital's chief doctor, called the *Oberartz*. She was frightened, certain that she had been found out. When she entered the office and saw the German town major standing next to the *Oberartz*, she became terrified. But to her surprise, the two men were smiling and congratulating her! They told her that she was to be honored with the German Iron Cross for her excellent work at the hospital in caring for both the German as well as the Belgian wounded.

In the autumn of 1915, around midnight, Marthe was walking as usual toward Number 63. She had a message to deliver: 1,000 German troops were all staying under one roof, at the Rousselaere brewery. She was just about to tap on the window when she heard footsteps behind her. Had she been followed? Perhaps it was another agent who used the same "mail bag" as she. Hiding back in the shadows, Marthe watched a dark form approach the window and heard a familiar series of taps. A hand reached from inside into the darkness. Suddenly, the shadowy figure pulled something from its belt and a gun was fired toward the outstretched hand. There was a sob, a scream, and then a thud. The dark figure opened the window higher and crawled inside. Marthe quickly slid past the window and reached her bedroom 10 minutes later in a trembling sweat.

Shaken as she was, Marthe realized that she still needed to get her message about the German troops at the brewery to British intelligence. Canteen Ma took the message from Marthe's mother and made sure it crossed the border.

That same evening Otto found Marthe in the café, took her by the arm, and led her into his apartment. Although Marthe knew he was a spy, she had almost lost her fear of him until that moment. But what he said surprised her. "Already you have gained the Iron Cross," he said. "Are you willing to work for the Fatherland—to gain even greater distinction?" He went on to say that he thought Marthe, with all her obvious intelligence, would be able to help him weed out the Belgian spies in Rousselaere. Desperate for a valid excuse to refuse, Marthe told him that she'd think it over.

Three nights later Marthe heard the drone of airplanes over-head followed by a series of thunderous explosions. Above the din she could hear the sound of human screams. She knew that the British bombers had struck their target: the brewery. And a half hour later, she began nursing the survivors when she was called to the hospital. She tried not to remember that she was partly responsible for all this suffering. She tried not to think of the wives, mothers, and sweethearts of the men who had just been killed. She forced herself to remember that "this was war."

The following day Otto pulled her aside and told her he was certain the bombing had been the direct result of a Belgian spy in Rousselaere. "I am going to get that spy, Marthe," he said. "I shall hope to hear that you have learned something within a week."

Marthe was terrified. Although she had no reason to suspect that Otto knew of her involvement in the brewery bombing, she was going to have to give him some information, some-thing that would not harm any Belgians but that would make it appear that she was willing to work for him. Otto was elated when Marthe brought him a fake message made from a non-sense code she had created but that she claimed to have found tied to the leg of a carrier pigeon. However, when Otto's profes-sional ciphers—code breakers—could make no sense of it, he became suspicious.

Marthe was frantic. The next morning she explained her pre-dicament to one of the safety pin men. Two days later, Otto was found dead, two bullets to his head. Marthe's terrifying career as a double agent was over.

One day in October 1916, several German nurses were sud-denly assigned to the hospital. They took an immediate dislike to Marthe and did whatever they could to hinder her work. Mar-the, obviously not wanting to be the center of attention, decided to resign. The *Oberartz* had tears in his eyes when he told her good-bye.

About a month later, Marthe was passing the town komman-dant's office when she saw a notice board listing a number of stolen items that had been retrieved from a thieving German soldier. One of the items listed was a watch with the initials M.C. Marthe had been missing just such a watch for a number of weeks. She went in to retrieve it. When she arrived home after several subsequent hours of shopping, her mother told her that the gendarmes had been there. An hour later, a strange man, speaking Flemish with a German accent, appeared at the back door of the café pretending to be part of the Belgian spy network. Then, that evening, one officer and two soldiers forced their way into the cafe and began a thorough, violent, and noisy search of Marthe's apartment above the cafe while she was forced to wait below. Suddenly everything above the stairs become very quiet. The officer came down triumphantly, holding two coded messages that Marthe had hidden carelessly. They arrested Marthe and took her to the military prison.

Although she was certain she'd be shot the following dawn, Marthe's trial didn't begin for several weeks. During that time of waiting she discovered what had tipped off the Germans: they had found her watch in the ruins of an ammunitions dump that Marthe and several safety pin men had dynamited just one month before. Her initials on the watch immediately caused her to come under a fair amount of suspicion, but when she came to claim it after reading the false story on the notice board, her connection to the explosion became clear. Lucelle's warning—"If you are caught, it will in all probability be your own fault"—now came back to haunt her.

While in prison, Marthe refused to divulge any informa-tion about the other spies in the network, although she was interrogated repeatedly. She had also determined not to say anything in her own defense at the trial. But as she looked around at the hostile faces of the Germans who were to decide her fate, she became filled with indignation and finally spoke. "I look on myself as a soldier in the field," she cried, "in face of an invader who . . . has made laws to suit his own convenience. You are Germans, I am Belgian . . . so in my own country it is perfectly legitimate for me to use every weapon in my power to defeat such an abhorrent machine which is attempting to overrun our beloved land."

The *Oberartz* of the military hospital then testified on Marthe's behalf, telling the court that she'd been awarded the Iron Cross. This seemed to make a profound impression on the German officers in the courtroom. Two other doctors testified on Marthe's behalf in a similar way. Her activities as a spy condemned her to death, but because of her work at the hospital, her sentence was commuted to life in prison. She spent two years behind bars before being liberated by British troops at the war's end.

Marthe received numerous honors from the governments of France, Belgium, and Great Britain. She married a British officer, John McKenna, and wrote her memoir while living with him in Belgium. When the Second World War broke out, the couple moved to England. She died in her hometown of Westrozebeke in 1966.

LEARN MORE

I Was a Spy! by Marthe McKenna (Robert M. McBride and Company, 1934).

LOUISE DE BETTIGNIES

Intelligence Organizer
Extraordinaire

"We have thousands of men to fill the vacant places in the trenches, but not many who could take your place. We have need of you."

—*Sir John French, commander of the British Expeditionary Force in France and head of the British armies in France, to Louise de Bettignies*

Beginning in August 1914, streams of French and Belgian refugees who had managed to escape the German invasion began to flood into Great Britain. But they weren't the only ones landing on British soil. German spies often tried to mix in with

Louise de Bettignies.
© *de Bettignies Archives*

the refugees. In order to weed them out, the British government quickly set up a system whereby, on first entering the country, refugees had to answer a series of questions from a panel of British officers and officials. This was not only an attempt to prevent German spies from entering the country, but also a way to discover what was happening in the German-occupied areas.

One day, early in 1915, a petite woman in her late 30s was on a boat approaching Folkestone, a frequent entry point on the coast of England. Though she understood the importance of the process that would await her there, she was concerned that it might slow her down, and she had a desperately urgent message to deliver.

She had been roused out of bed at 11:00 PM the night before by a man with terrible news. A French family had learned, through a German officer they had been forced to house, that the Germans were digging tunnels under a portion of the British trenches, which they planned to fill with explosives.

The woman immediately left Lille for England. She traveled all night across Belgium and made the dangerous crossing into the neutral Netherlands, where she was able to radio a warning message to British intelligence. But just to make sure it had been received, she boarded a boat bound for England.

When the ship arrived and the woman stepped onto the pontoon boat that connected to the shore, she was greeted by an English officer. He knew who she was and why she was there. "Madame," he said, "before your foot touches the ground, please accept the congratulations and the thanks of the British army that you have saved!" The British army had received the message, and the German plan had been thwarted.

This woman was Louise de Bettignies. Born in 1880 in Lille, France, into a poor but once noble family, Louise had managed to obtain an Oxford education and then had learned both Italian and German while working as a governess in Italy and Austria-Hungary. At one point she had received an offer from Archduke Franz Ferdinand, heir to the throne of Austria-Hungary, to become governess to his children, but she had refused: accepting the offer would have meant giving up her French citizenship.

She had been in France recovering from an appendectomy when the war began. She traveled back to Lille just before the Germans attacked and occupied her home city. Only part of France was still under French control, so many family members were now impossibly separated. People in occupied Lille were concerned that their relatives might take drastic, dangerous measures to discover what was happening to them beyond the German lines.

So they decided to create a "family post"—a mail delivery service for relatives—and Louise was chosen as the postman. Approximately 300 people from Lille gave Louise messages for their family members. She used lemon juice, an inexpensive invisible ink, to inscribe them all on a large petticoat. Upon arriving at her destination, she planned to iron the petticoat, making the messages visible, and then cut them out and mail or deliver each one to its recipients. Then she traveled across Belgium and the Netherlands, took a boat to England, and from there sailed for unoccupied France (the usual route followed during the occupation).

During this journey, she came into contact with officers of both British and French intelligence. When they discovered that she had successfully smuggled hundreds of messages out of occupied France in such a clever way, both organizations became anxious to recruit her. Louise loved the idea but was torn about which country to serve.

Before making a final decision, Louise sought advice from two people: her mother and a priest who had been her confessor before she became a governess. Her mother, who hadn't seen her since the invasion and didn't want to lose her again, tried to talk her out of it. Louise suggested they let the priest have the final word. Father Boulangé indicated that working for an intelligence organization was a different but valid way to serve God. He also pointed out that the French would probably not reimburse her until after the war whereas the British had said they would pay her up front.

Being a woman of modest means, Louise decided to work for the British: she would need money, not for herself but for those working under her and to pay bribes to German guards. And when she saw her mother again, this time she approved, saying, "My child, if it is your duty, do it."

Louise finished distributing her messages, loaded up a new petticoat with many replies for those in Lille, and then returned to Folkestone, England, for her training under the direction of Major Lord Cameron, known as Uncle Edward (the same officer who had trained Gabrielle Petit). Her alias was to be Alice Dubois.

Upon returning to Lille, Louise delivered the return messages she had and then conferred with Monsignor Charost, her current confessor. He confirmed the advice she had received from Father Boulangé and also gave her the names of people in Lille who were already working in some form of resistance. When Louise met them, they all became convinced that she was someone very capable of organizing and coordinating a successful network operation. The Alice Network had begun.

By the time Marie-Léonie Vanhoutte, a small, quiet woman from Roubaix, had been introduced to Louise, Léonie had already found a way to help her own brother escape from occupied France to the neutral Netherlands—a tedious and dangerous 65-mile trek on foot—so that he could serve in France's military against the Germans. She had traveled this route four times, helping other French servicemen in the same predicament.

Upon meeting Louise for the first time, Léonie had this reaction: "I . . . was ready to follow her anywhere, for I knew instinctively that she was a girl capable of great things." Léonie's alias was to be Charlotte Lameron, and she became "Alice's" lieutenant. Through Léonie, Louise was introduced to another man who would work with her closely, Victor Viaene, whose alias would be Albert. When he was first approached by Louise, he said, "One just had to follow her; it seemed impossible to refuse." Albert became a tireless courier and frequent traveling companion to the women.

There were hundreds of people involved in the Alice Network. Some of them were experts in particular fields, such as radio communications, chemistry, and photography, while others were ordinary people who discovered unusual but extremely effective ways to collect information. One of the most notable of these was Mme Levengle, whose window overlooked a train station. Since the Germans were touchy about French people who seemed too interested in the movements and number of German trains, she would sit in front of her window knitting, while tapping signals with her heels to her children in the room below. While they appeared to be doing their homework, they were actually jotting down the codes she was communicating, right under the nose of a German rail marshal whom they had been forced to house!

Others in the Alice network lived near crossroads and took note of passing military convoys. Some of them lived in or regularly visited areas where they could spot artillery positions, airfields, ammunition dumps, or amassed weapons. Those along courier routes offered their homes as resting places and hideouts. And guides helped couriers cross the Dutch border.

All the collected information would be dropped at "letter boxes" in various towns. Others would collect it and take it to Lille. There Louise would summarize the material into a report, translate it into code, and then, using durable ink, copy it in tiny letters onto special thin paper. This was a crucial step: except for identification papers, the Germans would not allow papers with printing or handwriting on them to cross borders.

When she was finished she would give the report to one of several couriers or sometimes carry it herself all the way to the Dutch border, often in the company of Léonie. She traveled four or five times alone to England. She also traveled in order to find more agents and visit the ones she had already employed.

Speed was essential since the information had to be given to the British while it was still accurate. The couriers mostly traveled on foot (occasionally in wagons), and, while Louise had been an excellent athlete as a student, exhaustion was a serious issue for most couriers. But it was not the only issue facing them. The Germans, in an attempt to keep all information about their activities from leaking to the Allies and to keep the occupied people in the occupied areas, had set up guarded checkpoints at the entrances and exits of all the larger towns. Travel from one of these towns to another usually required a special passport.

Yet even people with passports and proper identity cards—and Louise had many false papers identifying her as living in multiple areas—were searched. The Germans realized that there was espionage going on in the occupied areas, and they did their best to clamp down. Louise preferred to keep messages in her bag so they could be disposed of quickly in case of trouble. But this was dangerous. So sometimes the couriers, Louise included, would form a message into a ball attached to a thread: they could hold onto the thread while throwing the ball away and then follow the string back to the message. Other times Louise and

Léonie would slip their reports between the pages of a catalog. One day they dropped one, and a German ran after them, helpfully returning it. Louise would sometimes travel with multiple parcels and then open each one helpfully for the guard searching her until, exasperated, he would finally just let her pass.

After outwitting the guards, Louise would often whisper to Léonie, "They are too stupid. With any paper one sticks under their nose and plenty of self-possession one can get through." But the Germans were catching on. After British planes destroyed multiple specific targets, clearly the result of French espionage, couriers for the Alice Network had to become ever more creative, hiding their reports in umbrella handles, bag handles, garment hems, shoelaces, and heels of shoes.

While Louise was very good at planning things ahead of time to avoid danger, she could also think very quickly on the spot when necessary. If a guard seemed suspicious, she would sometimes smile and tell him an amusing story in German, which generally put him in such a good mood that he would let her through. On one occasion, she convinced a particularly obnoxious woman sentry—known as "the Frog" because of her special green uniform—to believe she had been desperately trying to hide a sausage. The Frog confiscated it and began eating it, but Louise's bag was completely overlooked.

Louise treated these incidents as if they were a game. When Léonie tried to warn her to take them more seriously, Louise replied, "Bah! I know I'll be caught one day, but I shall have served. Let us hurry, [Léonie], and do great things while there is yet time."

The dangers she faced were not only the German guards at town checkpoints. Wanting to keep people from crossing into the Netherlands, the Germans had installed powerful searchlights in certain places along the Belgian-Dutch border, along with armed guards who were ready to shoot anything they saw moving. Nearly every morning the area would be littered with the bodies of dead men, women, and children.

Louise sometimes passed under the searchlights too. She would wear light clothes and walk directly under the lights. She believed, correctly, that the people who were shot had been given away by their shadows: the farther away they were from the searchlights the longer their shadows became.

The Germans also laid mines in a wooded area near the border. One day, while walking behind a couple approaching the Dutch border, Louise saw them step on a mine and explode right in front of her. Passing their mangled bodies filled her with horror, but she continued on her way. Speaking later of the incident she said, "Danger does not frighten me, but I do not like to see it."

Was Louise de Bettignies ever really frightened? "Yes, just like everybody else," she admitted, "but only after the danger was past; before then it is an indulgence."

One day, after she and a companion had successfully fooled a guard at a checkpoint (with the help of several young boys who passed an ID card back to one woman after the other had used it first), two men approached and asked the laughing women for their identity cards.

"But we showed them over there," Louise protested.

"Show them again," one of the men demanded.

"Who are you?" Louise asked.

"German authority," he said, pulling out a medal.

Louise was arrested and, when incriminating evidence was found on her, she was eventually taken to the Saint-Gilles prison, where Léonie Vanhoutte was also held, having been arrested a few weeks earlier.

After spending about five months in jail, Louise was tried in court and given a death sentence. Upon learning a short time later that her sentence had been commuted to life imprisonment, she smiled and said, "Until France is victorious." But to Léonie she said, "I have a feeling I shall never return."

She was right. After serving two years in Siegburg—a German prison where she was instrumental in leading a strike against the guards for forcing the female inmates to make munitions for the Germans—Louise died on September 27, 1918, after complications from an operation, conducted in the filthy prison and without anesthetic, to remove a cancerous tumor.

The Alice Network had provided extremely valuable information to the Allied cause. A member of the British intelligence interviewed after the war said, "The services Louise de Bettignies rendered are inestimable. Through her we learned with a precision, a regularity, and rapidity that was never surpassed by any other organisation, all the movements of the enemy, the exact position of their batteries, and a thousand details that were of great help to our headquarters. Possibly, during the course of the war, experience having perfected the method of working, one or two services equaled hers. Not one has ever surpassed it."

LEARN MORE

The Queen of Spies: Louise de Bettignies by Major Thomas Coulson (Constable, 1935).

The Story of Louise de Bettignies by Antoine Redier (Hutchinson and Company, 1924).

PART II

MEDICAL PERSONNEL

"Faster than women can save, men go out and kill."

—Madeleine Zabriskie Doty, American
writer who toured wartime Germany

"Think of all the youth, the blooming youth and powerful manliness that lies here destroyed. Father, Father, can this truly be the will of God?"

— Käthe Russner, German surgical nurse who worked
on the western front, in a letter to her father

Approximately 10 million military men were killed during the war. That number would have been much higher if it hadn't been for the medical personnel who worked as near as they were allowed to the fighting lines. Hundreds of thousands of these medical workers were women, some of whom took on various roles such as doctors and ambulance drivers. However, this type of work was still generally considered somewhat inappropriate for females, even in wartime, and the women who filled those positions were far outnumbered by men doing similar work.

But the one role for women that was given the official stamp of approval by most nations involved in the war, and which was therefore filled by enormous numbers of women, was that of the nurse.

During the 18th and 19th centuries most battle-wounded men of Europe and North America had been cared for by overworked male orderlies, but there had often been women tending their wounds as well, many of them medically untrained "camp followers." These women suffered from generally bad reputations among those outside of the military, either because some of them weren't actually married to the soldiers they had followed into battle or simply because of their unchaperoned proximity to so many men.

This negative perception of women in the role of battlefield nurses began to change during the 19th century because of the efforts of some key women to improve the quality of military nursing. The most notable of these was British nurse Florence Nightingale, who tended the wounded of the Crimean War of 1853–56 and wrote an influential book on her findings.

While her ideas were generally taken seriously, it wasn't until the end of the 19th century that the notion of professionally training large numbers of young women to fill the role of military nurse became generally accepted throughout many countries. During the Boer Wars (fought between Great Britain and the descendants of Dutch colonists living in South Africa from 1880 to 1881 and from 1899 to 1902) and the Spanish-American

War (fought between Spain and the United States in 1898), more men died of diseases contracted while waiting in filthy conditions for medical treatment, than from their actual wounds.

And so, in the years just prior to World War I, hospitals in countries such as Canada, Australia, Great Britain, and the United States began to run increasingly professional nursing schools. Eager young women flocked there by the thousands, becoming the core of trained nurses during the war.

Once the war began, the large number of casualties made it clear that even more nurses were needed, so quicker nurse training was instituted in many countries. For instance, before the war, there had been fewer than 4,000 nurses in the Russian Red Cross. These nurses had trained for one year; but shortly after the war began, the Red Cross training period was shortened to two months and later—when more volunteers were needed and included—to six weeks. By the end of 1914, 10,000 Russian

Empress Alexandra and her older daughters, center, wearing nurse uniforms. Like most women of the royalty and nobility, the empress actively supported her nation's wounded during the war. However, Alexandra went further than most other female royals who donned Red Cross uniforms: she often assisted surgeons during serious operations. *Great War Primary Document Archive, 2367*

nursing students were studying at 150 Red Cross schools, and by 1916, these schools had produced approximately 25,000 nurses.

There were thousands of volunteer nurses in other combatant countries as well—about 92,000 Germans and 60,000 French women served, and between 50,000 and 70,000 British women worked as Voluntary Aid Detachment (VAD) nurses. Whether they received payment or worked voluntarily, many of these nurses signed up for what they thought would be the greatest adventure of their lives, especially those from Australia, Great Britain, Canada, and the United States, most of whom were sailing away from home for the first time. Some of the professionally trained nurses were also able to take pride in the fact that they could now join nursing organizations that had in recent years been made official parts of their countries' armed services.

"If we had been nursing strange troops we may have felt it less, but among our own people the horrors of war are brought home more intensely. Almost everyone on the ship has some relation or friend at the front & so you are constantly dreading to hear the latest news, in case it is some one we know."

—Alice Kitchen, Australian army nurse,
writing during the Gallipoli campaign

But in all the combatant countries that utilized female nurses, there was still a widespread concern about young women having close contact with wounded men. The nursing uniforms did much to counteract this worry. Partly because nuns had historically been heavily involved in caring for the civilian sick, most uniforms for military nurses created during the late 19th century resembled nuns' habits. Composed of multiple layers of cloth, these uniforms were designed not only to protect the nurses from disease but to place an emotional barrier between the female nurses and their male patients. And the nurses were referred to as "angels of the battlefield" in France, "sisters of mercy" in Russia, and "nursing sisters" nearly everywhere else.

Even if romantic connections were discouraged, soldiers and their nurses—many of whom worked in medical establishments that largely supported the men of their own countries—shared emotional bonds that were not forbidden. Wounded men arriving at these medical care stations, having previously lived for long stretches of time exclusively in male company, were very glad to be assisted not only by women but by fellow citizens. Their presence was a powerful reminder of the soldiers' prewar lives.

Nurses often saw their duties to their fellow countrymen as being directly patriotic: serving the medical needs of their own country's soldiers was a way of serving their country. And while many nurses worked in hospitals that were far from the fighting, those who worked closer to the battlefields were the first to either grieve for or glory in the military activities of their fellow citizens.

"This has been a dreadful time at Passchendaele & our Canadian boys have done wonderful feats of endurance & fighting against almost impossible odds."

—Clare Gass, Canadian nurse on the western front,
diary entry for November 5, 1917

More than 3,000 nurses served in the Canadian Army Medical Corps (CAMC) during the war. Most of those who went overseas nursed the wounded among the approximately 600,000 men of the Canadian Expeditionary Force, which made significant contributions to the Allied cause on the western front. *George Metcalf Archival Collection, © Canadian War Museum*

For all their training, most nurses—or any other medical personnel supporting the war, for that matter—had not been prepared for what they had to face when they encountered the war's first wounded. Expecting much tidier wounds, they scrambled desperately to learn new techniques with which to help men who had parts of their faces missing, their legs smashed, or gaping holes in their abdomens that exposed their organs.

"The very word 'wounded' is enough to strike horror to the heart of anyone who has seen a shipload of 'wounded' arrive."

—Narrelle Hobbes, Australian nurse who tended to the wounded of the Gallipoli campaign

The Weapons and Wounds of the Great War

"These shells make a most horrible scream before bursting, like an animal in pain."

—Violetta Thurstan, British
nurse on the eastern front

While machine guns, rifles, grenades, and mortar bombs caused innumerable deaths and maimings, the most disfiguring wounds of the war resulted from shrapnel caused by exploding shells fired from cannons.

Because artillery shells were so effective, they were used frequently, especially just before an infantry (foot soldier) attack. The deafening and repetitious sound (and feel) of the cannons firing at regular intervals over no-man's-land caused some men so much tension that they developed a psychological condition referred to as "shell shock." While the onset of this malady can be traced to other sources—many other aspects of the war caused this type of damage as well—it is clear that artillery was the weapon that caused the most physical and psychological damage throughout the war.

The nurses were often extremely overworked, in some cases because military commanders had not accurately predicted the numbers of men who would need medical attention. This was particularly true in poorly planned battles during the initial years of the war, such as the one fought on Gallipoli Peninsula in the Ottoman Empire. Troops from Britain, France,

Australia, and New Zealand (the latter two forming the new Australian and New Zealand Army Corps, the ANZACs) attempted to open a waterway to their Russian ally by disembarking from ships sailing into the Ottoman Empire's Dardanelles Straits. The Allied invaders and the Turks, determinedly defending their homeland, were both killed in enormous numbers.

Australian casualties of Gallipoli being transported to a hospital ship.
Australian War Memorial

"There must have been a shocking lot of casualties at the Dardanelles by the accounts we hear. . . . The hospital ships provided were not nearly sufficient for the number of wounded to be transported . . . but the staff, of course, was nothing like adequate for the work. We have so little time to talk to the men & occasionally hear some of the details; some were shot in the boats before they landed at all."

—Alice Kitchen, Australian Army nurse

Did the nurses working near the battle zones come under fire? Yes. If the wounded were to survive, they needed medical care as soon as possible, which meant that nurses came as close to the fighting as they were allowed. On the western front, where the lines of battle were relatively permanent, the medical stations were too, and the nurses there—at first—kept some distance from the fighting.

As the war progressed, however, and the nurses' presence at medical stations closer to the front became necessary, many western front nurses faced increasing danger, although never as much as their counterparts working on the eastern front's constantly shifting lines of battle.

"A very fierce German attack was going on, and the bullets were pattering like hail on the trees all around us. We could see nothing for some time but the smoke of the rifles."

—Violetta Thurstan, British nurse on the eastern front

Despite the horrific wounds inflicted on the battlefields of World War I and the enormous numbers of men who lost their lives quickly—or slowly and painfully while waiting in vain to be rescued—a large percentage of wounded men who received immediate medical attention actually recovered. If it hadn't been for the medical personnel who worked tirelessly to save them—many of whom lost their own lives in the line of duty— the death toll during the war would have been much higher.

ELSIE INGLIS

Surgeon and Hospital Founder

"In Scotland they made her a doctor; in Serbia we would have made her a saint."—*Serbian saying regarding Elsie Inglis*

Dr. Elsie Inglis refused to retreat. *Not this time.* She was in Kruševac, Serbia, at one of the hospitals she had created. She had recently been persuaded to leave critically ill patients during a retreat, and although they had been left in the hands of a competent Serbian doctor, Elsie's decision still haunted her.

Now she witnessed the final retreat that would be forever after known in Serbia as the Great Retreat. The promised help from Serbia's allies was clearly not going to come. There was no longer any hope of holding the country from its enemies,

Elsie Inglis in 1916.
Dr. Elsie Inglis (1919)

who were now invading landlocked Serbia from all of its borders but the southwestern one. The Serbian army was about to do the only thing left: take a dangerous winter journey on foot with the few supplies they could muster through the Albanian mountains to the southwest. Many civilians, including staff from Elsie's hospital, accompanied them.

On November 6, 1915, Elsie and the others who had chosen to remain in the hospital in Kruševac felt a great explosion. It shattered the windows in the hospital and in the house where the medical staff lived. A train loaded with ammunition had been blown up by the retreating Serbs, who couldn't take it with them across the mountains, to keep it from falling into the hands of the enemy. The Germans retaliated by bombarding the retreating Serbians. The Germans would be in Kruševac the following day. Dr. Elsie Inglis was determined to be there when they arrived.

Elsie Inglis had always been strong-minded. She was born in 1864 to Scottish parents who held the opinion, unusual at the time, that the education of a girl was just as valuable as that of a boy. Elsie grew up wanting to become a medical doctor. Although this was nearly unheard of, there was a growing need for female doctors: many Victorian-era women put their lives in jeopardy because they were embarrassed at the thought of being examined by male doctors. Because of this problem— among other reasons—women in the United Kingdom finally won the right to obtain medical degrees in 1876; and in 1886, the Edinburgh School of Medicine for Women was established. After graduating from this institution in 1892, Elsie focused her time and energy on two basic issues: the plight of the poor and the oppression of women.

Treating the poor, often for no pay and well beyond the call of duty, brought Elsie much praise from the communities she served. One man said that Elsie had "done more for the folk

living between Morrison Street and the High Street [the poor
section of the city] than all the ministers in Edinburgh and
Scotland itself ever did for anyone." As a practicing physician
in these neighborhoods, Elsie also became acutely aware of the
need for greater rights for women. Married women were not
allowed to have surgeries unless their husbands gave their official permission. They didn't always give it. Some men would
take their wives home from the hospital just as they were being
prepared for serious and necessary operations, often giving no
valid reason for their interference. These injustices fueled Elsie's
desire to work for women's rights, and she became the honor-
ary secretary of the Scottish Federation of Women's Suffrage
Societies.

When the war began, Elsie looked for a way to involve herself in medical war work. Although her surgical experience had
been mainly in women's medicine, she realized that there would
be a tremendous need for surgeons during wartime and every
willing doctor could certainly find a way to help. In September,
she went to the Edinburgh branch of the Royal Army Medical
Corps (RAMC) to offer her services to the British army. She was
turned down with these words: "My good lady, go home and sit
still." But Elsie didn't want to go home, and she certainly wasn't
going to sit still.

Instead, she had a startlingly new idea: she would create a
mobile hospital unit staffed and run entirely by women. She
suggested it to the executive committee of the Scottish Federation of Women's Suffrage Societies. They loved it. Not only
would such a hospital make a valuable contribution to the war
effort, but its success would prove the value of female doctors.
After being told by Sir George Beatson, the head of the Scottish Red Cross, that the British Army would reject the idea,
Elsie wrote letters to the ambassadors of Belgium, France, and

Russia, asking if their governments would be interested in having a fully staffed mobile hospital to serve their wounded. The answers came in: yes.

The Scottish suffrage society's offices in Edinburgh immediately became the headquarters of what would be called the Scottish Women's Hospitals for Foreign Service (or the SWHs). They ran an advertisement in the journals of the National Union of Women's Suffrage Societies, and Elsie made impassioned speeches before large audiences: "The need is there," she pleaded, "and too terrible to allow haggling about who does the work." The money came pouring in.

One hospital was established in France and a second in Kragujevac, Serbia. Elsie was busy in Britain with the organizational and fund-raising needs of the hospitals, all the while yearning to be working in one herself. Her opportunity came when the chief medical officer in Kragujevac became seriously ill and Elsie replaced her. By the time Elsie arrived in Serbia, in May 1915, there were four SWH units in the country. The SWH in Kragujevac was running three separate hospitals: one for surgeries, one for victims of a typhus epidemic that had begun in the winter, and one for general disease.

By July the typhus epidemic was largely under control. During this somewhat peaceful time, Elsie tried to persuade the local Serbian authorities in the four nearby towns that housed SWHs that their water supplies should be better protected to avoid the spread of epidemics. The Serbians took Elsie's warnings to heart and, on September 7, a new stone fountain in Mladenovac was dedicated to Elsie and the SWHs in Serbia in a formal ceremony attended by local dignitaries and Serbian officers.

The Austrians—this time joined by the Germans—were clearly mobilizing for a third attempted invasion of Serbia during the summer of 1915. Serbia's eastern neighbor, Bulgaria, was promised postwar territory by Germany and in September decided to join the Central Powers. With Serbia's allies nowhere in sight (in spite of their promises), the Central Powers could now easily invade Serbia and take hold of the Serbian section of the trans-European railway; this would link Germany to its ally Turkey, making the transportation of weapons, supplies, and men easier. Germany, Austria, and Bulgaria all mobilized for a Serbian invasion. Belgrade, Serbia's capital and largest city, fell on October 8.

When Elsie, whose Kragujevac hospital was flooded by the Belgrade conflict's wounded, received orders on October 23 to retreat, she was very hesitant. Twenty patients were too ill to be moved. Elsie could only be persuaded to leave after she had explained their cases in detail to a Serbian doctor who was going to stay behind. But she left with a heavy heart, vowing that she would never again leave her patients to face the enemy. Shortly after she set up a new hospital in the town of Kruševac, word came that the Serbians—civilians and soldiers—were going to retreat through the Albanian mountains. Staff from the Scottish Women's Hospital had a choice: leave and risk the freezing mountains or stay and face the invading enemy. Elsie and a number of other hospital personnel chose to stay.

When the Germans arrived a few days later, Elsie was initially impressed with their polite courtesy. They even complimented her on the quality of her main hospital. But it soon became quite clear who was in charge. They demanded that all the Serbian patients be removed from the main hospital. They eventually made Elsie and her staff leave it too, although they had initially been allowed to stay because they were caring for the German wounded. When Elsie protested this treatment to the Serbian hospital director, he replied, "But of course they took it. You had made it so beautiful."

The hospital that was allowed to treat the Serbians was called the Tsar Lazar. It soon became seriously overcrowded. Elsie and her staff of 20 washed, ate, and slept in a single room. Elsie could never forget the typhus epidemic that had greeted her upon her arrival in Serbia, and she knew current conditions at the Tsar Lazar—overcrowding, intense cold, lack of fuel and food—were now ripe for another epidemic. But Elsie and her staff worked so hard at disinfecting the patients and their surroundings that they had only one case of typhus while the enemy hospital was rumored to have many.

Toward the end of November, after securing the railway to Turkey, the Germans planned to depart from Kruševac, leaving occupation duties to the Austrians. But before they left, a German army doctor asked Elsie to sign a paper certifying that the Germans had all behaved well while occupying the area. It was just a formality, he told her, a simple request.

While it was true that Elsie had been pleasantly surprised by the generally polite manner of the Germans—so vastly different from the reports she'd previously heard of their behavior in Belgium—she and her staff *had* been forced out of their own hospital into dangerously crowded conditions. The Germans had also prevented the women from receiving any outside information. In other words, they had been prisoners. Elsie decided that signing the document would give a false impression. She sent a message to the army doctor: she wasn't going to sign. An angry message came back. The German high command in Berlin was very displeased with her refusal. She *would* sign the certificate, the officials insisted. If she continued to refuse, her entire hospital unit might be forced into Germany.

"If it is a matter of no importance," Elsie replied, "I fail to understand why the High Command should know anything about the matter or why it should make them angry. But if it is an affair of sufficient importance to interest the High Command, I wish to know just why it is important, before I sign."

She wasn't given an answer but was asked twice more to sign, the final time in a room full of German officers. The commanding officer, leaning over the table across from Elsie in a threatening manner, said to her, "Sign at once. I will make you."

"Make me," she replied. Then she closed her eyes, awaiting the worst. There was silence for several long minutes. When Elsie opened her eyes, the commanding officer was still looking at her. Then, without a word, he signaled one of his aides to take Elsie from the room.

Later, when asked if she'd been afraid at that moment, she said, "Afraid? How could I be, with the whole weight of the British Empire behind me? It was a great day in my life when I discovered that I did not know what fear was."

While some members of the medical unit took up an Austrian offer of repatriation at the end of December—they would be peacefully returned to Great Britain—Elsie and a few others chose to stay as long as possible. Most of their patients had been evacuated, but more were coming. And Elsie still believed the Allies might come to help Serbia after all. But she eventually realized that this was a false hope. She agreed to leave at the beginning of February.

When she arrived back in Britain, Elsie finally discovered why the Germans had been so determined to have her sign the paper: it was to offset the outrage caused by the German execution of nurse Edith Cavell in October 1915, one month before they had pressured Elsie. If Elsie, who was well known in Britain, had claimed the Germans had treated her well, it might have helped counteract the current negative worldwide image of the Germans caused by the Cavell execution.

Most of the repatriated medical personnel took a vacation on their return to Britain, but Elsie didn't. She went to the British War Office and asked about the possibility of setting up a Scottish Women's Hospital in Mesopotamia, where the British were fighting. As a response, she got a rude runaround. Finally, though, she was able to set up a SWH destined for Russia that would support a Serbian army division attached to the Russian army.

In October 1917, it was decided that the remaining Serbs being treated in Elsie's SWH would be evacuated to Great Britain and that Elsie's hospital would leave as well. The journey home, by train and boat, was a grueling one not only because the Russian Revolution made part of the journey very dangerous; Elsie had realized months before that she had cancer, and she was now in the last painful stages of the disease. Although the hospital staff she had been working with knew she was very ill, none of them knew specifically what was wrong or how close to death she was. When she died on November 27, 1917, the day after reaching Great Britain, some of her British associates were still wondering which train she would arrive on.

The Scottish Women's Hospitals had begun with the idea of raising £1,000 for the creation of a single mobile hospital. In the end, a total of nearly half a million pounds was raised. That money was used to create 14 hospitals that served the wounded in France, Serbia, Romania, Russia, Malta, Corsica, and Macedonia.

Thousands of Britons and nearly every Serb then living in Britain attended Elsie's funeral. In 1925, the Elsie Inglis Memorial Maternity Hospital was founded in Edinburgh. Four years later, in Belgrade, Serbia, another hospital would bear Elsie's name.

In 1916, Elsie had become the first woman to receive Serbia's highest honor: the Order of the White Eagle. She was so beloved in Serbia for many years following her death that a famous saying about her circulated there: "In Scotland they made her a doctor; in Serbia we would have made her a saint."

LEARN MORE

Dr. Elsie Inglis by Lady Frances Balfour (George H. Doran Company, 1919).

Elsie Inglis: Founder of Battlefront Hospitals Run Entirely by Women by Leah Leneman (NMS Publishing, 1998).

Shadow of Swords: A Biography of Elsie Inglis by Margot Lawrence (Michael Joseph, 1971).

OLIVE KING

Adventurous Ambulance Driver

"That first winter in Salonika was a never-to-be-forgotten time of mud, floods, discomfort and hard work. All the same it was real good fun."—Olive King

Olive May Kelso King was born in 1885 in Sydney, Australia. But in the summer of 1914, when the war broke out in Europe, she was visiting her older sister Sunny in England. Olive's father, a wealthy Australian philanthropist, had always encouraged Olive to travel (well chaperoned, of course) each time he suggested she break off her latest unsuitable romantic attachment.

In spite of having attended a German finishing school for young women, Olive's real interests were all considered dis-

Olive King wearing the uniform of a Serbian army ambulance driver.
Australian War Memorial

tinctly masculine at the time: not only could she drive an automobile but when her father sent her to Mexico in 1910, Olive—accompanied by several male companions (only because her chaperone was safely in their hotel room with a bad headache)—became the third woman to climb the volcano of Popocatépetl, the second-highest peak in Mexico, and the first woman to descend into its crater.

When Britain declared war on Germany, and Australia enthusiastically pledged its army to support Britain, Olive decided that this war would be her next great adventure. Like most people at the time, she thought it would be over in a matter of months. She saw it as a way to express her strong sense of pride in being part of the great British empire. But she had a deeper motivation too: she longed to do something significant. In 1913, she had written a poem called "Cry of a Starved Woman" in which she had asked God to "send me a sorrow . . . to waken my soul from its engulfing sleep." Perhaps she would find what she was longing for by becoming involved in the war.

But what would her particular involvement be? She decided to train as an ambulance driver. Because the British army had already purchased most of the available ambulances in Britain, Olive bought a used lorry with funds provided by her father and had it converted into an ambulance. She called it Ella the Elephant because it was so large (it could hold 16 seated patients) and so heavy. After some training, she joined a volunteer organization, the Allies Field Ambulance Corps (AFAC), and then crossed the English Channel with her ambulance, winding up in Belgium. Shortly after her arrival, the AFAC organizers, who were suspected by local authorities of espionage, fled the country. Olive and two Canadian women drivers were forced to find their own way back to England, just ahead of the invading German army.

Olive King with her ambulance in France.
Australian War Memorial

Back in England, Olive joined the Scottish Women's Hospitals for Foreign Service (SWH), an organization run and staffed by women. As soon as she passed tests in both driving and the French language, she was accepted into an SWH unit that was stationed at Troyes, France, attached to the French army.

In the spring of 1915, Olive began to realize that the war would not be over as quickly as she had once thought. On a train traveling the first leg of a trip that would take her unit from France to the Balkans, Olive wrote to her young stepmother, "I sometimes feel . . . as if this rotten war were going on for ever. Every few weeks it seems to increase rather than slacken off, more countries getting dragged in."

The unit's trip aboard a boat called *Mossoul* from Marseilles, France, to the port of Salonika, Greece, took more time than usual because the sailors were trying to avoid German submarines; another hospital boat supporting the Allies had been torpedoed and sunk by the Germans just before arrival on November 3, 1915.

Olive's unit eventually erected a field tent hospital close to enemy lines in Gevgeli, a town on the border of Greece and

Greece During the Great War

Greece was officially neutral during the first year of the war but switched its stance several times in the years that followed. Why? While its prime minister, Eleftherios Venizelos, was pro-Allies, the loyalties of King Constantine I were with Germany. He had been educated there and was married to the sister of Kaiser Wilhelm.

When Greece's neighbor Bulgaria joined the Central Powers in October 1915, Prime Minister Venizelos invited the Allies to make Greece a base of operation. But when the Allies began arriving the following November, they were received coldly by the pro-German king and his government, which had just removed Venizelos from office. Lacking an army large enough to force the Allies from his shores, however, Constantine could only reestablish official neutrality. But in June 1917, the king—having lost his protection as a fellow royal from the Russian tsar, who had been forced to abdicate the previous March—was forced into exile. Venizelos, who in 1916 had managed to establish his own separate government in one section of Greece, now took control of the entire country. Greece declared war on the Central Powers and actively supported the Allied cause throughout the rest of the war.

Serbia. The hospital had 300 beds but was treating nearly 700 patients. Olive and the other staff members worked for 16 to 20 hours a day in difficult conditions, including short rations and freezing weather. One day the unit received an urgent message: Bulgarian troops, who had a reputation for brutality, were headed in their direction. The Bulgarians had just pushed back a corps of French and British soldiers and the Serbian army, which the medics had come to support, was retreating from its own country. Thirty women, assisted by 40 Royal Engineers (who had been stranded in the area), were given less than 24 frantic hours' notice to dismantle the entire hospital unit before the area would be overrun by the enemy.

While 13 French ambulance drivers who had been supporting the hospital decided to take a slow retreat down a rickety trek, most of the staff and patients were able to evacuate aboard the trains that were leaving Gevgeli. Olive and two other female drivers didn't join them; they couldn't bear to leave their vehicles to the Bulgarians or to destroy them to prevent this from happening. Trains that clearly had room enough for the ambulances pulled into the station, one after another, but the women were always told that while there was room for them, there was no room for their trucks.

Finally, the last train leaving Gevgeli pulled into the station. The Bulgarians were now less than half a mile away. Without asking permission, the women drove their trucks onto the train. A few minutes after the train pulled away a Bulgarian shell destroyed the station where Olive and the others had been waiting. Later, Olive heard that the 13 French ambulance drivers had been captured and killed by the Bulgarians.

Back in Salonika, where the Allied armies were regrouping, the staff set up another hospital in the midst of a very wet, muddy winter. Olive was very busy but in a mundane sort of way. She wrote to her father that her real dream was to be "in the thick of things." She was also growing tired of how the hospital matron seemed to be more interested in rule enforcement than in making the workers feel appreciated. And Olive's new romance with a Serbian officer—Captain Milan Yovitchitch—was beginning to clash with the SWH's close supervision of its off-duty employees. So in the summer of 1916 Olive quit the SWH and joined the Serbian army as an ambulance driver attached to medical headquarters. She moved into an apartment with two other female ambulance drivers who had also just left the SWH.

Olive had been happily working for the Serbs for several months when she was stricken with a serious case of malaria. Milan was at her side daily, and when she recovered they were closer than ever, working together near the front lines of battle, where Olive transported men and supplies in her truck.

On Serbian Easter Sunday of 1917, the Serbian army made Olive a sergeant. At this point, Olive was not only in love with Milan but with all the Serbs. She explained in a letter to her father, "I always feel one can't do enough for them, after all they have suffered to keep their word with us. Our own Tommies [British soldiers] have so much, they don't need the little one could do for them, & wouldn't appreciate it in the same way that the Serbs do."

On the afternoon of August 17, 1917, a fire broke out in Salonika, which was now swarming with soldiers from Serbia, France, Britain, Russia, and Italy, as well as colonial troops from India, Indochina, and North Africa. Olive, seeing the fire from a distance and longing to have a closer look, was thrilled when she was ordered to assist. Driving into the city she found it a place of utter confusion as panic-stricken people fled with whatever goods they could rescue from the terrifying roar of the flames.

Olive, at times only yards away from the fire, worked all night rescuing people and their possessions. Moments after one Serbian family climbed into her ambulance, their house caved in with a deafening crash. Olive kept saying to herself that it was all "too dreadful . . . too frightening to be really happening." She also worked to keep the Serbian army's supplies from going up in flames by helping the others lay protective wet tent material over them. Stopping only at 4:00 AM for some sleep, she worked long hours for the next two days, transporting refugees throughout the demolished city. It took two weeks to completely quench the fire. By that time 80,000 Salonikans had lost their homes. For her conduct during the fire, Olive was highly honored by the Serbian government, receiving both a Silver Medal for Bravery and a Gold Medal for Zealous Conduct.

In the fall of 1917, it seemed that Olive was sent the "sorrow" she had requested in her 1913 poem: Milan left Serbia in order to work at the Serbian embassy in London. Olive knew that their relationship—begun in the unnaturally intense climate of war—was over. To counteract her deep sadness, Olive plunged herself into the task of helping others, first obtaining food for the mechanics attached to the Serbian army and then assisting the Serbian soldiers and thousands of homeless people in Salonika by way of mobile canteens that were supplied through funds by Australian donors who had been contacted by Olive's father.

Olive then found a way to bring these canteens to Belgrade, Serbia's capital city. The Allies finally helped the Serbs make an advance into Serbia in late 1918, pushing the Central Powers out of the country, and Olive followed with her canteens. Not only were the Serbs starving because the retreating troops had destroyed everything in their wake, but transportation lines had also been devastated and desperate vandals were everywhere.

Nevertheless, Olive managed to open and run multiple canteens in many additional Serbian cities.

Only after the last canteen closed in 1920 did Olive finally return to Australia, where she became state secretary and then assistant state commissioner of the Girl Guides (Australian Girl Scouts). When Australia became involved in World War II and Olive volunteered to drive for the Australian army, she was told that, at the age of 55, she was too old. So after studying at an aircraft school, she became a quality examiner at an airplane factory.

She and Milan remained friends and corresponded for many years. She kept a photo of him, dressed in a Serbian officer's uniform, in her bedroom. He married someone else. Olive never married. She died in Melbourne, Australia, in 1958 at the age of 73.

LEARN MORE

"King, Olive May (1885–1958)"
Australian Directory of Biography
http://adb.anu.edu.au/biography/king-olive-may-6962
Written by Hazel King.

The Beauty and the Sorrow: An Intimate History of the First World War by Peter Englund (Knopf, 2011) contains sections on Olive King.

One Woman at War: Letters of Olive King, 1915–1920 edited by Hazel King (Melbourne University Press, 1987).

HELENA GLEICHEN

X-Ray Expert on the Italian Front

"We are cleverer than the English then, because we employ who and what we can for our wounded, regardless whether they wear trousers or petticoats."

—Italian Duke of Aosta on the hiring
of Helena Gleichen and Nina Hollings

"We are lucky to be right in the thick of it like this."

—Helena Gleichen

It was November 1916. The Italians had already lost tens of thousands of men during their battles with the Austrians along the Isonzo River, the main area of the Italian front. But

---

Helena Gleichen.
Contacts and Contrasts (1940/2013)

the recent sixth Battle of the Isonzo—otherwise known as the Battle of Gorizia—had been different. Although just as costly as the previous battles in terms of the loss of Italian lives, this conflict had provided the surviving Italians with an enormous boost in morale: they had finally been able to take Gorizia, a city within the border of Austria-Hungary that was home to many ethnic Italians. Capturing this territory was part of the reason the Italians had entered the war.

The enormous number of Italian casualties from that battle had kept radiographers Helena Gleichen and Nina Hollings frantically busy as they tried to assist the surgeons in locating deadly pieces of metal embedded within the bodies of wounded men.

But the fighting continued, so the women were still working hard several months later as they attempted to cross the Isonzo River on their way to a hospital on the other side. They were stopped by Carabinieri (Italian police) who told them that the bridge was being shelled and was too dangerous to cross. As the women waited in their transport, chatting with others who were also waiting by the riverbank, an orderly suddenly came running through the crowd shouting, "Badly wounded men at the head of the bridge—is there an ambulance?" Someone needed to be willing to turn around and take the wounded men away from the river to the nearest field hospital.

The women turned to the ambulance driver standing next to them. He shook his head: his transport was already full. There were no other suitable transports available in the crowd except for the women's car. Without further hesitation, they quickly emptied it of their precious X-ray equipment, asking a soldier to watch over it while they were gone. The shells headed for the bridge were increasing. Nina went to see if she could help with another wounded man waiting near the river as Helena tried to turn their car around. She managed to do so just as eight wounded men—two of them serious "stretcher cases"—were shoved into the back of the car.

Racing through the twisted road back into Gorizia, Helena and the wounded passed some men on mules and horses who shouted, "You can't pass this way! The road is being shelled!" But one of the seriously wounded men was bleeding so badly he would die if he didn't receive immediate medical care. What could Helena do?

There wasn't much in the upbringing of Lady Helena Gleichen that would have seemed to prepare her for such critical decisions. Her father had been born Prince Victor of Hohenlohe-Langenburg (a tiny German kingdom), a favorite nephew of Queen Victoria (through her half-sister), for whom he was named.

When Victor married Laura Seymour, a beautiful young woman from an aristocratic British family, his own family (including his aunt, the queen) was opposed to the match. Hohenlohe-Langenburg law forbade any of them to marry beneath their exact rank, and Laura's didn't match his precisely. When Victor, in love with Laura, decided to marry her anyway, it was declared a morganatic marriage: his wife and children were forbidden to share in or inherit his titles. When Laura was given the name Gleichen (instead of Hohenlohe-Langenburg), Victor also changed his name to Gleichen.

The queen eventually accepted the couple, and the Gleichens' three daughters and one son grew up in Saint James's Palace in London, England. The daughters were encouraged by their parents to seek an education and a profession "as if [they] had been boys," which was very unusual for the time. The youngest Gleichen daughter, Helena, became a professional painter.

When the war started, Helena looked for a way to help the war effort. She began in 1915 as an ambulance driver in a British hospital in France, where she and Nina Hollings—her close friend whose son had died in France in the fall of 1914—also worked as translators between the French patients and their British doctors and ran a dispensary for sick civilians.

A French surgeon visiting their hospital had been very impressed with the women and suggested that they consider learning the relatively new science of radiography, an activity

Marie Curie and Radiography During World War I

X-rays had been discovered by Wilhem Röntgen in 1895, but a woman was responsible for first bringing them to the front lines of World War I. Marie Curie, a two-time Nobel Prize recipient for her scientific breakthroughs in the fields of physics and chemistry, realized that many lives could be spared if X-ray equipment—already found in hospitals far from the front—could be utilized near battle zones, where doctors often wasted precious time searching unsuccessfully—and painfully for the patients— for bullets and shrapnel fragments inside wounded men.

She pressed through the many bureaucratic obstacles placed in her way before seeing to it that stationary radiography units were installed in field hospitals while mobile units—referred to as "petite Curies"—were used closer to the front lines of battle. Marie personally trained many of the radiographers who worked during the war, including her own daughter. Because of Marie's efforts, more than one million wounded men were X-rayed during the war.

he told them was "very badly needed" by the Allies on the western front.

Helena and Nina liked the idea. They studied radiography in Paris for six months, obtaining official certificates before working in London under a well-known British X-ray specialist so they could learn his methods as well. Meanwhile, their wealthy relations raised funds to purchase portable X-ray equipment that the women could transport to dressing stations and field hospitals near the front lines of battle.

Italy and the Great War

Since 1882, Italy had been officially allied with Germany and Austria-Hungary in what was referred to as the Triple Alliance. But when Germany and Austria-Hungary declared war on the nations of the Triple Entente (Russia, France, and Britain) and requested that Italy do the same, Italy refused, claiming that their alliance did not require Italy to follow the other nations into war. The underlying reason for Italy's refusal, however, was Italia Irredentia ("unredeemed Italy")—territory that lay within the borders of Austria-Hungary but was inhabited by many ethnic Italians—which Italy wished to acquire. So when the nations of the Triple Entente asked Italy to join their side, Italians in the government saw it as a way to gain the lands it wanted. On April 26, 1915, Italy officially left the Triple Alliance, and on May 23, it declared war on Austria-Hungary.

But when they offered their services to the British War Office, they were refused on the clumsy (and clearly false) grounds that "no women had ever been known to be radiographers." The French War Office, while accepting their offer, gave them the runaround—and then the French Red Cross stole their equipment after the women had showed them how to use it!

After Helena and Nina chased down and retrieved their equipment and while they were wondering what to do next, an acquaintance told them he thought the Italians would be glad to have them.

In December 1915, Helena and Nina arrived in Italy. They were given several rooms—cold and without real beds—within a large villa that had been vacated by an Austrian count who had immediately fled when the Italians had entered the area.

During their first night in Italy, Helena was sleeping when she noticed that the far-off noise of the artillery had changed to the sound of rifle and machine-gun fire that suddenly seemed "suspiciously close." She tried to go back to sleep, assuming that such noises were usual in a war zone.

In the morning, she discovered that the sounds she had heard weren't necessarily normal for that area: during the night the Austrians had come very close to the villa—firing from about two miles away. As alarming as that was, it would not be the women's closest brush with danger during their time in Italy.

The women were both given the rank of majors in the Italian army and initially traveled to 11 different field hospitals as well as multiple dressing stations. Their equipment was hooked to a power generator located in their car. They would use it to locate the bullets or pieces of shell that were embedded in the wounded men. Working from what they could see on their screen, they would make two marks on a wounded soldier's skin—one on his front and one on his side, the bullet or shrapnel piece being

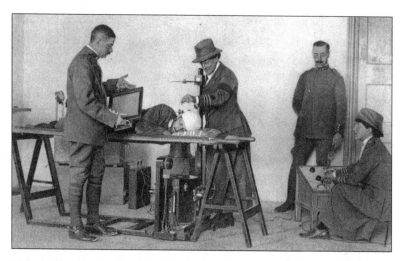

Helena Gleichen and Nina Hollings at work.
Contacts and Contrasts *(1940/2013)*

located at right angles to the two marks. Although the ideal way
to perform radiography was to make a permanent "plate" of each
patient, the enormous number of wounded men needing X-rays
made this impossible. Instead, Helena—who had studied anat-
omy as part of her art training—would often copy the results of
their findings from the screen onto a piece of paper. Her drawings
were usually accurate, and the surgeons found them very helpful.

For the cases where permanent pictures *were* necessary, the
women would develop plates in the dark room of their living
quarters, working late into the night. An orderly on a bicycle
would then deliver the developed plates to the pertinent field
hospitals early in the morning so the surgeons could use them
during operations.

Helena and Nina were able to help wounded soldiers in sometimes dramatic ways. One day they were asked to see a man
whom the doctors thought had lost his mind. Thanks to an X-ray
of his skull, surgeons were able to remove a piece of shell that was

pressing on his brain. On another occasion, the women located a shell fragment near the eye of a man who had been blinded. The surgeons removed it, and the man's sight was restored.

But often what appeared on the screen could only make clear that a man was going to die. This was particularly true when the women encountered their first poison gas victims.

Poisonous gas had been used on the western front since the spring of 1915, but to the men on the Italian front, the gas warfare being waged in France sounded like a story whose dangers might be slightly exaggerated. Although the Italian troops had been supplied with gas masks, which they carried in their pockets, they had not been carefully drilled on how to use them during a gas attack. So when the first such attack came, they were unprepared.

When Helena and Nina received the call to help gas victims at a dressing station, their way inside was blocked by a courtyard filled with gassed men, many of them already dead. The surgeons, desperately curious to view the lungs of a gassed man under the eye of the X-ray, asked the women to X-ray one of the dying men. The screen showed a pair of lungs that had shriveled to about two inches in diameter.

At this point the women were visiting 27 different hospitals and various dressing stations as well. Many of these dressing stations were difficult to find as the Italians were trying to keep them hidden from the Austrians.

On their way to a station hidden in a narrow mountain valley, a shell fell very near Helena and Nina's car, landing by the side of the road in deep mud before exploding and covering the car with mud and stones. Then another shell fell behind them.

When they arrived at the dressing station, the surgeons told them that earlier they had noticed an Austrian plane flying back and forth very low over the station. Through binoculars, they had been anxiously watching the women approach and were certain their car had been hit by shrapnel. Helena and Nina had actually been discussing this as they approached. Nina, who had been sitting in the back of the car, was certain they had been hit, while Helena was just as certain that they hadn't. Everyone at the station began to question why the Austrians would be wasting their time shelling such a small area so far behind the lines, which contained only wounded soldiers. As they talked, several more shells hit nearby.

The women had been called there to X-ray a man with a head injury. But when they began to use the equipment, it suddenly stopped working. They ran outside, where the motor was, to see what was wrong. One of their helpers was under the car and showed them that Nina had been right: their equipment had been hit—and a wire severed—by a piece of shrapnel very close to where Nina had been sitting.

On their way out of the valley the Austrian shells continued to fall around them, one of them dropping just behind their car. They both heard the gunfire, heard the whine of the shell coming closer and closer, but they continued at the same speed. Why? Slowing down or driving faster was useless since they had no idea exactly where a shell was going to land. So "not looking at each other or daring to speak," they drove on. A shell fell behind their car, creating a huge crater in the section of road they had just passed.

In August 1916, during the attack on Gorizia, the women had to deal with many spinal injury cases. Most of the time they discovered via X-ray that pieces of shrapnel had passed through the spine. The women knew that it would just be a matter of time before these men died.

As sad as some of their cases were, in order to do their job well, Helena and Nina had to focus on the work and not let their emotions get in the way. Writing home, Helena described their work environment in this way: "The bustle and noise, the groaning, the cries for 'Mamma mia,' the smell of disinfectants and the smell of blood all help to make the place a nightmare, never to be forgotten, but the work has to be got through in double-quick time, as more and more men are being carried in and more are expected."

Then one day in November 1916, because she was willing to transport some seriously wounded men stuck at an impassable bridge on the Isonzo river, Helena found herself racing from a heavily shelled bridge to a heavily shelled road. But she felt she had no other choice: one of the men was bleeding to death.

The car went faster than Helena believed possible, and she got the men to the hospital in time. Then she drove back to the bridge, where she found Nina with the equipment (the wounded man Nina had been attending to there had died), and they both drove across the bridge.

The women's work had by this time become very well known, and shortly after Helena's heroic drive, an officer escorted the women to the opera house in Gorizia, a large and beautiful building that had huge holes in its roof caused by shells.

As the women were escorted to their box, decorated with both English and Italian flags, the officers in all of the boxes—all representing the various regiments of soldiers who had taken part in the Battle of Gorizia—stood up and saluted while the soldiers below stood at attention. Through the holes in the roof, the women could see the planes that had been ordered to guard the opera house during the ceremony.

Many *Medgalie al Valore Militare*—medals for military valor— were given out that morning to various Italian heroes of the Battle of Gorizia. When it came time for the women to receive their medals, the general turned to their box and said, "Soldiers here present, we greet these two English women whom we look upon, not only as two of our most gallant officers, but as beloved members of our families, and we offer them, and ask them always to wear the medal we have had struck for all the officers who took part in the victory of Gorizia."

Helena and Nina left Italy in October 1917. The Italian army continued fighting the Austrians, suffering—and causing— enormous losses without gaining much territory until the decisive Battle of Vittorio Veneto, fought in October and November of 1918. When the Austrians began to surrender by the hundreds of thousands rather than fight, their generals could do nothing but ask for an armistice, which they did on October 29. The Italians ignored it and kept fighting. The second time the Austrians asked for an armistice, on November 3, it was accepted by the Italians and signed that same day.

Nina and Helena lived together for a time after the war in a large manor in Great Britain until they had to give it up for financial reasons. Both women were granted the Most Excellent Order of the British Empire, the OBE. During World War II, Helena organized a Home Defence Corps of 80 people. She died in 1947, a few days before her 74th birthday.

LEARN MORE

Contacts and Contrasts by Helena Gleichen (John Murray, 1940; reprint Mansion Field, 2013).

The White War: Life and Death on the Italian Front, 1915– 1919 by Mark Thompson (Faber and Faber, 2008).

SHIRLEY MILLARD

Nurse Armed with Enthusiasm

"Banners streamed in my blood. Drums beat in my brain. Bugles sounded in my ears. I wanted to go overseas."

—*Shirley Millard*

To young Shirley Millard in March 1918, New York City seemed to be the most exciting place on earth. The United States was on the verge of sending large quantities of trained troops overseas, and young men in uniform swarmed the city, marching in parades and crowding into the Red Cross centers and canteens.

Why had the United States joined the war? President Woodrow Wilson had been determined since the war's outbreak to

A group of American volunteer nurses on their way to France.
Marion McCune Rice Collection © Steve Hooper

117

stay neutral. In fact, his 1916 reelection slogan had been, "He kept us out of the war."

But Germany, having been pressured by the United States in 1915 to stop its submarine warfare against nonmilitary vessels, now thought that using U-boats to sink all ships traveling in and out of British ports might be the quickest way to win the war. When unrestricted submarine warfare officially resumed in February 1917 the Germans sunk an American ship, and the United States broke off diplomatic relations with Germany. Soon afterward, the American public discovered the existence of the Zimmerman Telegram, a communication sent to the Mexican government from a German official in which he promised to give US territory to Mexico if Mexico would join the Central Powers. When three more American ships were sunk by German submarines in March 1917, President Wilson could no longer avoid a decision to join the Allies. On the evening of April 2, 1917, he gave a speech to Congress saying that war with Germany was necessary, not because the United States wanted more territory like most of the European combatants but because "the world must be made safe for democracy." Congress agreed, and on April 6, 1917, the United States was officially at war with Germany.

However, at the time, the United States had a very small army, especially in comparison with Germany's, and it took some time for the United States to prepare enough troops to send across the Atlantic.

So nearly a year later, in March 1918, many of the young men Shirley personally knew were either being trained, waiting to leave for Europe from New York, or already in France. Everywhere she went, Shirley heard patriotic, pro-war songs being sung and played: "Over There," "It's a Long Way to Tipperary," and "Roses of Picardy." Shirley became desperate to go overseas.

Over There

When the United States declared war on Germany, George M. Cohan, an American performer, composer, and Broadway producer, locked himself in his New York office until he had finished a song that he titled "Over There." It became wildly popular—selling more than two million copies of sheet music and one million records before the war's end—and was powerfully influential in stirring up the patriotic fervor that led thousands of young American men and women to enthusiastically support the war against Germany. In 1936, US president Franklin D. Roosevelt awarded Cohan the Congressional Medal of Honor for "Over There" and another patriotic song, "You're a Grand Old Flag."

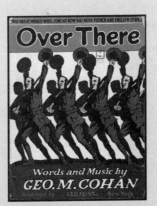

"Over There" sheet music cover.

Over there, over there
Send the word, send the word over there
That the Yanks are coming, the Yanks are coming
The drums rum-tumming everywhere.
So prepare, say a prayer
Send the word, send the word to beware.
We'll be over, we're coming over
And we won't come back till it's over, over there.

She imagined herself in the midst of noble and heroic activities: driving an ambulance in the line of fire, rescuing men stuck in no-man's-land, or bringing comfort to the wounded and maimed. There was only one problem: Shirley had no medical training. But when she discovered that France's nurse shortage was so desperate that they were accepting untrained American nurse volunteers, nothing could stop her. And so, armed only with her enthusiasm and an ability to speak French, she sailed to France with a volunteer medical unit of 10 nurses.

When Shirley and the unit arrived in France, they were told they were to be rushed to an emergency hospital that had been set up quickly close to the French defense line on the grounds of a chateau. "We are all thrilled to have such luck," Shirley wrote in her diary. "Real war at last." They arrived just as darkness was beginning to fall. Covering the grounds of the chateau, outside the hospital barracks, were what appeared to be sleeping men. Shirley soon discovered that these were the wounded who had been transported from the battle and left alone on the grounds until someone could help them or, in many instances, discover whether they were alive or dead. Many of these men had already been waiting for hours—often days—on the battlefield and received only whatever simple treatment could be given to them in rudimentary dressing stations directly behind the trenches. They had to wait there until nightfall when it would be safer to drive to better-equipped hospitals like the one Shirley had been assigned to.

She never forgot the first moment she entered the hospital barracks and went on duty: "Inside, all was confusion, disorder and excitement. Only dim flickers from candles illumined the chaos. Nurses, doctors, orderlies, beds everywhere; yet not nearly enough to take care of the influx of wounded.

"Stretcher bearers perspired under their loads until the aisles of every ward were packed. And still the grounds outside were full to overflowing. In the darkness under the trees orderlies stumbled about, giving a hurried drink to parched lips that had cried for water for twenty-four hours."

Shirley and the other volunteers had been promised some basic medical training from the hospital chief, but the huge influx of wounded caused by this major new German offensive left no time for training. As someone thrust equipment into her hands and began giving her orders, Shirley watched and imitated a more experienced nurse. She learned quickly how to prepare the wounded soldiers for their operations by giving them a tetanus shot and then removing their clothing and whatever bandages had been applied at the dressing stations. The wounds were horrific: "Gashes from bayonets," she wrote. "Flesh torn by shrapnel. Faces half shot away. Eyes seared by gas; one here with no eyes at all. I can see down into the back of his head. Every now and then the pit of my stomach sinks. I set my teeth and go on. A chest ripped open exposes lungs working feebly and slowing down under my very eyes."

The surgeons were always exhausted. One day she saw one of them—Dr. Le Brun—holding on to the door of the operating room, swaying from fatigue, and saying to himself, "La gloire, la gloire! Bah! C'est de la merde!" [Glory, glory! Bah! It is crap!]

By April 1, 1918, the German push had diminished, and the medical personnel finally had some time to organize the wounded into wards according to their medical issues: spinal injuries, gangrene, gas burns, meningitis, fractures, and what had suddenly become the largest number of cases—influenza. Half the men at the hospital who caught influenza died from it.

Shirley was out walking with Dr. Le Brun one day when some Americans marched by, on their way to the front. "They were grinning like pleased youngsters on the way to a picnic," Shirley wrote.

The Influenza Pandemic of 1918

The influenza epidemic of 1918 began, most likely, in March at a military training outpost in Fort Riley, Kansas. It quickly turned global, infecting approximately 500 million people worldwide and killing between 50 and 100 million, both soldiers and civilians—more than were killed from direct war-related causes. It was referred to as the "Spanish flu" because neutral Spain's government (unlike those of the combatant nations) allowed its newspapers to honestly report the epidemic's initial deadly effect. The particular strain of this flu was highly unusual because a large percentage of its victims were young and otherwise healthy. This had a direct affect on—and was directly affected by—the war: armies were suddenly depleted, and infected soldiers spread the illness when traveling by troop trains to various hospitals. While Germany, with its weakened economy and malnourished civilian and military population, was especially hard hit by the epidemic, all the armies of the war were affected. More US soldiers in Europe died of the flu than were killed in combat.

"Le B. remarked as they passed that one could see the difference in temperament between the French *poilu* [soldier] and the American doughboy [the term for US soldiers in WWI] by the way they wear their helmets. The French plant theirs solidly on their heads, having learned from bitter experience that this is where they will do the most good. But our boys still wear theirs cocked jauntily over one ear."

The United States Military Contribution to the War

Great Britain and France perceived the allied US troops who came to France in large numbers during the spring of 1918 as too late, poorly trained, and led by men dangerously uninterested in the knowledge that had already been painfully acquired on the western front. Nevertheless, the stream of these enthusiastic American soldiers seemed endless to the German troops, who were accustomed to fighting the depleted and war-weary British and French soldiers they had come close to defeating in the preceding months. When the Germans clashed with the Americans in several key battles in 1918, the numerous and motivated Americans often destroyed the confidence of the German soldiers along with their will to fight.

Nursing Americans shifted Shirley's perspective on the war. The men she was trying to help were no longer only those of a foreign nation; these were her fellow citizens and she was proud of them. "Such gallantry, such nerve, such pluck!" she wrote, describing them in her diary. "Even the French nurses have remarked about it. Always: Thank you, for every little thing. And: How soon will I be able to go back to the line? And: Help him first, he has waited longer than I have. I feel they are mine, every last one of them, and their downright grit makes me want to cry all over them."

One day Dr. Le Brun's surgery nurse fainted from exhaustion. All of the other surgical nurses were busy. Shirley had hoped to assist surgeons but so far had not been allowed, so she now offered her services to Dr. Le Brun. When he waved her off impatiently, she asked him if he would please give her a chance.

He then asked her, "somewhat wearily," if she knew the French names of the more than 100 surgical instruments that he used routinely. She didn't. Dr. Le Brun turned and walked away. Shirley followed him, promising that she was willing to learn. He told her that she would have to learn immediately if she was to replace the other surgical nurse. She made sketches and took notes as the doctor showed her each instrument, including "knives, scissors, saws, pincers and dozens of little probes and mallets."

She took her notes and went on a walk. "Never had I studied a French lesson so avidly or so thoroughly," she wrote. Two hours later, she passed the "test" with Dr. Le Brun. "Bien, bien! Allons-y! [Good, good! Let's go!]," he said.

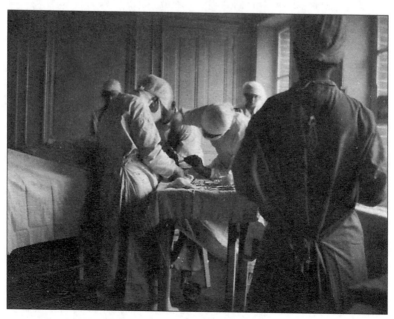

A French surgeon being assisted by American nurses.
Marion McCune Rice Collection © Steve Hooper

One day, after Shirley had been assisting him for several hours, she saw Dr. Le Brun staring at the face of their next patient, an unconscious man. His lower jaw was gone. His tongue was gone. But the rest of his face seemed strangely familiar.

Suddenly, Shirley and Dr. Le Brun looked at each other sharply. Without saying a word, they both realized that the man before them was Dr. Le Brun's handsome young friend René, whom Shirley had met briefly several months earlier when he had come to the hospital for a visit. His body was covered with wounds, and one leg was completely crushed. Shirley fought back tears. Dr. Le Brun cursed in French. Shirley poured him a glass of cognac. He drank it silently and then stared at René, clutching the sides of the table with his hands. Then he began asking for the instruments and went to work, his teeth gritted during the entire operation, his voice harsh when he called for the anesthetist.

René died without regaining consciousness. Dr. Le Brun did not operate any more that night.

After Shirley was relieved of surgery duty, she was placed in a ward called the *salle de mort* ["room of death"], where the wounded were brought when it became clear that they would not survive. One of the men was an American sergeant named Charley Whiting. A bullet through his spine had left him almost completely paralyzed and unable to speak more than two whispered words at a time. He communicated for the most part using his facial expressions and two fingers that he could move slightly. He generally only used these difficult forms of communication to thank the nurses for everything they did for him.

But one day he tried to tell Shirley something different. "My mother . . ." is all he could say. Shirley responded by asking if he wanted her to write to his mother. He did. Shirley agreed, although she had no idea what she could possibly say. "My heart is sick over the thought of the letter I must write," she noted in her diary.

Charley died on the morning of November 10. Shirley held his hand while he died. That same day the nurses were told that the armistice would become official the next day. When one of them came to tell Shirley that the hospital staff had opened some bottles of champagne and were drinking it in the dining hall, Shirley told her to get out. "All very well to celebrate," she wrote, but "there is no armistice for Charley or for any of the others in that ward." She was relieved the war was over, but her heart felt "heavy as lead."

She finally found the words to write to Charley's mother as she made preparations to leave. Then she and the others from her unit were formally thanked for their service in a speech from the hospital chief with what seemed to Shirley at the time to be "a jumble of empty words." During her stop in Paris she received a response from Charley's widowed mother, forwarded from the chateau; the letter informed Shirley that Charley had been engaged to be married. His mother wrote that both she and Charlie's fiancée were very grateful that there had been "someone good and kind to take care of him to the last."

Charley's mother went on to say that she had given Shirley's letter to the editor of the local paper because she "was so proud of all the things you said about my boy." Then she added, "Perhaps you will have a son of your own some day. Then you will know how much they mean to us. I can only pray God there will never be another dreadful war like this has been."

But during the mid-1930s, when Shirley suddenly encountered her forgotten war diaries in a storage trunk, the world was "once again beating the drums of war," and Shirley had a five-year-old son named Coco. When she decided to publish her diaries, she dedicated the book to Coco, "his friends and their mothers." *I Saw Them Die: Diary and Recollections of Shirley Millard* was published in 1936.

LEARN MORE

I Saw Them Die: Diary and Recollections of Shirley Millard by Shirley Millard, edited by Adele Comandini (Harcourt, Brace and Company, 1936; reprint Quid Pro Books, 2011).

PART III

SOLDIERS

"Once at the front, I forgot whether I was a man or a woman. I was just a soldier."

—Arno Dosch-Fleurot, member of the
Russian Women's Battalion of Death

"'Do you like short hair?' I asked her.
'For a woman, no. For a soldier, yes,' she answered."

—Bessie Beatty, American reporter, interviewing a
member of the Russian Women's Battalion of Death

When the war began, and the governments of the combatant countries started their propaganda campaigns equating patriotism with military duty, some women took it to heart in a way that hadn't been intended: they wanted to become soldiers. Although their governments provided many other ways for them to support the war effort, some women were determined to accept nothing less than participation in direct combat with the enemy.

"I want to shed my blood for the fatherland, to give my life for my homeland!"

—Sofia Pavlovna Iur'eva, Russian woman, at the war's outbreak

---

There was only one problem with this ambition: except for some unique situations during the war, women were not recruited, trained for, or generally wanted in this role. As a result, the number of women involved in actual combat was relatively small—though the exact number is unknown since many of them most likely died and were buried without their gender ever being discovered.

But the stories of these women soldiers are fascinating for a number of reasons. Not only are their determined personalities very compelling but their stories also provide a slightly different perspective on—and open a unique window into—the world of male soldiers.

What was combat like for a soldier of the Great War? The nature of the fighting differed on the war's various fronts, but a large percentage of soldiers spent long periods of time in trenches, areas that were built (or more accurately, dug) right on the lines of fighting. Battles on the eastern front, fought largely between Russia and Germany, were usually conducted from trenches that were relatively shallow and temporary, reflecting the lines of battle that shifted depending on the outcome of the most recent conflict. The trenches on the Italian front were made of mud or stone. And the most elaborate—and permanent—series of trenches were those that ran along the western front, a battle line that stretched from Belgium all the way through France.

Military leaders on all sides considered trench warfare to be a temporary situation necessary only until one side or the other could gain the upper hand. So their men waited in the muddy, unhealthy, lice- and rat-infested living areas, sneaking out occasionally into no-man's-land for raids and sniper fire while both sides battered each other with artillery.

"The dirt, the flies, the vermin, the monotonous round [of artillery] . . . the waiting—these are the things that take the last ounce of a man's courage and faith."

—Bessie Beatty, American reporter with the
Russian army on the eastern front

Meanwhile, their leaders made plans for battles they were convinced would break the deadlock. Their basic strategy was taken from wars of the previous century in which the amount of courage shown by individual men participating in offensive attacks could make the difference between victory and defeat.

Although the new means and methods of World War I made these charges impractical, most military commanders at the time were convinced that offensive attacks were still the most effective way to wage war. So they sent wave after wave of soldiers charging bravely toward the enemy during the major battles of the war, believing that victory would come to the army that possessed the most courageous men.

But no matter how determined or brave a soldier was, he couldn't repel bullets being rapidly fired from a machine gun, nor could he walk through barbed wire—the two major defensive weapons of the war—through the sheer force of his personality. The major battles of the war yielded enormous body counts of men who had rushed "over the top" (out of the trenches) to their deaths.

"I asked one man who came in from the front where he had come from & he said he thought it was from 'Hell.'"

—Alice Kitchen, Australian army nurse

Although the soldiers of certain nations had specific motivations for fighting—invasion of their homelands, for instance, in places such as Turkey, Belgium, Serbia, and France—many of those who had eagerly signed up for military service early on were convinced it was going to be the greatest adventure of their lives. After the devastating reality of the war had stripped it of any excitement, what kept the men charging out of the trenches to their deaths? Often it was the fear of being thought a coward by their comrades-in-arms (or possibly even worse, by themselves); the dread of public corporal (physical) punishment; or the possibility of a death sentence. But in the latter years of the war, many military commanders had to deal with men who mutinied against their leaders, openly revolting in enormous numbers. Even the most patriotic soldier became weary of following orders in a war that seemed to have no reason and no end in sight.

"They were not individual Russians any longer, they were just soldiers; they were not men who were going to die for their country, they were just men who were going to die."

—Marina Yurlova, female Russian soldier

In spite of all the difficulty and danger, there were hundreds—possibly thousands—of young women who were determined to join the ranks of the fighting men, most of them disguising their gender in order to do so. When these women were wounded and their gender was discovered, what happened next depended on the country. The British, French, and German women warriors who attempted to sneak into their country's ranks were rarely allowed to stay and fight, but some notable women were allowed to serve openly both in the armies of Austria-Hungary and Serbia.

Milunka Savić, Serbian woman warrior of both Balkan wars (1912 and 1913) and World War I, and one of the most highly decorated women in military history.
Courtesy of the Military Museum in Belgrade

But the nation that had by far the largest number of women soldiers was Russia. Close to 1,000 Russian women fought alongside men, even before the Russian Provisional Government (see sidebar on page 140) began actively recruiting women soldiers.

Many Russian men viewed women as equals on a certain level, despite the many laws in the country that limited the rights of women, one of which forbade them to attend higher education without the permission of either their fathers or husbands. But female and male rural peasants—the largest Russian population group—had always equally shared the grueling labor necessary for survival. And Russian folklore was filled with physically strong female characters.

"Women can fight. Women have the courage, the endurance, even the strength, for fighting."

—Bessie Beatty, American reporter in Russia

And so, when a Russian woman was found among the fighting men, she was often allowed to stay in the ranks but was sometimes transferred to a supportive role rather than an active one. Russian women near the front lines often worked in dangerous reconnaissance missions (gathering information from enemy territory), transporting ammunition, or as stretcher bearers, rescuing wounded male soldiers out of no-man's-land.

Some countries that would not allow women to participate in direct combat did provide official supportive military roles for them during the war. For instance, in 1917, the British government created the Women's Army Auxiliary Corps (later Queen Mary's Army Auxiliary Corps), the Women's Royal

US Navy yeomen.
National Archives 165-WW-598-B-1

Naval Service, and the Women's Royal Air Force. The women who filled these positions replaced men who were then freed to serve in active duty.

Two British organizations—the Women's Emergency Corps and the Women's Volunteer Reserve—went a step further by training the women in their ranks to use weapons in case Great Britain was invaded. Australia had a similarly militaristic organization for women: 700 women were part of the Australian Women's Service Corps. Although the women in these organizations practiced and drilled as if preparing for active military duty, they were never actually involved in combat.

When the United States became involved in the war, its navy became the first American organization to grant women full military rank and status. In the spring of 1917, when male navy "yeomen"—clerks who performed secretarial duties—were required for active duty, Josephus Daniels, secretary of the US Navy, asked (in a line that was to become famous): "Is there any regulation which specifies that a navy yeoman be a man?"

His own answer to that question was a decided no. And within a month 200 women had become navy yeomen, to a loud outpouring of criticism—from everyone from the navy's own board of legal advisers to newspapers throughout the country. However, Daniels not only stood by his decision but went a step further: he insisted that women receive equal pay for equal work, a highly unusual idea at the time. By the end of the war approximately 11,000 women had become navy yeomen.

MARIA BOCHKAREVA

Women's Battalion of Death

"The soul of the army is sick and we must heal it."

—*Marya Skridlova, member of the*
Women's Battalion of Death

On July 9, 1917, the 525th Regiment of the Russian army crouched in the trenches. Looking across 800 feet of no-man's-land, they could see movement in the German trenches. They were awaiting orders to charge. Their mission? To capture specific territory held by the enemy in the forests of Novospasskii and Begushinskii along with some nearby villages. The regiment had waited through a tense night. At three o'clock in the morning, the order to advance finally came—but no one

Maria Bochkareva.
Library of Congress, LC-DIG-ggbain-26866

Battalions and Regiments

A battalion is an army unit consisting of 300 to 1,000 soldiers. A regiment is usually two battalions.

moved. The officers begged their men to act, but they refused. The debate between the officers and their men dragged on for hours, but nothing was decided. The ideal time for an attack was quickly passing.

Suddenly a large group of women in soldier's uniforms, accompanied by 75 male officers and 300 fighting men, leapt from the Russian trenches and charged toward the German line, all of them running straight into a hail of enemy bullets.

These women had been waiting long enough. Part of the Women's Battalion of Death, they had trained intensively for a month of 16-hour days. And although their charge into German fire was the first active military experience for most of them, it wasn't the first such experience for their leader, Maria Bochkareva, an illiterate peasant woman who had been an active participant in the Russian army since the beginning of the war.

In the summer of 1914, 25-year-old Maria—who had already survived an abusive childhood and two violent romantic relationships as a young woman—was on the point of suicide. When the war began, she was suddenly energized by the idea of taking an active military role in Russia's defense. "Our soldiers were retreating in some places and advancing in others," she said later. "I longed for wings to fly to their help."

When she tried to enlist in a reserve battalion in her hometown, the commander told Maria that it was illegal for women to fight at the front but that she was free to join the Red Cross or work in some other auxiliary, supportive service. But Maria would not be dissuaded from her desire to fight with the men, so the commander suggested that she appeal directly to the tsar, the official head of the Russian armed forces. When Maria agreed to try this, the commander helped the illiterate woman compose a request to send to their monarch via telegram.

The tsar responded positively, allowing Maria to begin military training with the men of the Fourth Company of the 25th Tomsk Reserve Battalion. She quickly earned their respect because of her excellent marksmanship.

Maria's unit was sent to the Russian western front in February 1915. Most of the regular soldiers there didn't take issue with her gender, but some of the officers did. They couldn't argue with a decision made by the tsar, however, so Maria was sent to the trenches with the others. Because of her consistent courage under fire, in the course of nearly two years Maria earned several military honors and military rank promotions, authority over a group of 11 men, and three hospital stays for battle wounds.

When Maria and the other soldiers heard about the February Revolution in 1917, they had a number of different reactions. Nearly all were relieved that the oppressive tsarist state had been overthrown, but many reacted to the democracy now granted them by the Provisional Government (with pressure from the Bolsheviks) by losing all interest in the war. Others, like Maria, were convinced that their new freedom only increased their responsibility to protect Russia.

Maria's opinion was in the minority. She was on the verge of leaving the army in disgust when she met Mikhail Rodzianko, the former head of the Duma (part of the tsarist government), who was on a mission from the Provisional Government to

The Russian Revolution

The Russian Revolution consisted of two main events: the February Revolution (named according to the Julian calendar Russia used at the time; it was March 1917 according to the western calendar) and the October Revolution (November 1917 using the western calendar). The February Revolution began with civilian rioting in Petrograd over severe shortages in food and fuel caused by freezing conditions during the winter of 1917. The people blamed the war and Tsar Nicholas II—a man ill-equipped for a job he clearly never wanted. When he was forced to abdicate, the tsarist government was replaced by the Provisional Government, which became engaged in a struggle for power with its rival, the Petrograd Soviet, which was eventually controlled by the Bolshevik political party. The October Revolution was the overthrow of the Provisional Government by the Bolsheviks, who took Russia out of the war. Years of civil war followed, fought between the Bolshevik "Red Army" and the anti-Bolshevik "White Army." The Bolsheviks won in 1922, establishing Soviet Russia, which became the largest member of the new Union of Soviet Socialist Republics, the USSR.

boost morale among the soldiers at the front. When he met Maria, he realized that this battle-scarred, highly decorated woman might be an effective propaganda tool to continue Russia's involvement in the war. He escorted her to various military meetings in Petrograd, Russia's capital city. It was during this time that Maria proposed an idea to Rodzianko: the formation of an all-female battalion that might shame male Russian soldiers into continuing the fight.

With official approval from Alexander Kerensky, the minister of war for the new Provisional Government, Rodzianko began a publicity campaign—including many impassioned speeches from Maria—that was designed to attract volunteers to the new women's military unit, referred to as the Women's Battalion of Death. Nearly 2,000 enthusiastic women, ranging in age from 18 to 35, responded, at least half of them educated professionals.

"Men and women citizens! Our mother is perishing. Our mother is Russia. I want to help save her. I want women whose hearts are loyal, whose souls are pure, whose aims are high. With such women setting an example of self-sacrifice you men will realize your duty in this grave hour! Women, do you know what I have called you here for? Do you realize clearly the task lying ahead of you? Do you know what war is? War! Look into your hearts, examine your souls and see if you can stand the great test."

—Excerpt from one of Maria's recruiting speeches

Maria was burdened with a tremendous sense of responsibility for making the battalion a success, so she trained the women very seriously. Recruits rose at 5:00 AM and trained until 9:00 PM. And since she had become a successful soldier in the Imperial Army by behaving like a man, Maria thought that suppressing femininity and mimicking masculine behaviors was the only way to make good soldiers. To encourage this transformation, Maria insisted that the women shave their heads. She taught them to smoke and swear. Giggling and smiling at male instructors were grounds for dismissal. Her sense of rigid authoritarianism was also something she'd learned in the tsar's army. But the ideals of democracy that had swept into Russia with the February Revolution had suddenly made authoritarianism very unpopular.

However, Maria stubbornly refused to allow the creation of democratic soldiers' committees within the battalion—although many military officials pressed her to do so—because she believed that democracy had destroyed the effectiveness of the Russian armed forces. Her demand for absolute obedience caused many of the women, especially the educated, to leave the battalion within the first few days. Maria was soon left with approximately 300 enlistees. But she didn't care about numbers: she prepared to train these women, whom she knew would follow her without question.

A section of the Women's Battalion doing a physical drill.
Blood Stained Russia (1918)

The women's battalion had enemies. The Bolsheviks realized that the battalion was a propaganda tool being used to continue a war that they claimed was an imperialistic conflict that had heartlessly sacrificed the uneducated peasant class only to benefit the rich. The Bolsheviks wanted Russia to pull out of the war so that a civil war—one that they would initiate—between these two classes could begin and enable them to seize control of the government. The women of the battalion were also harassed so much by male soldiers in their own units that they finally posted round-the-clock guards at their training barracks to protect themselves from disturbances that often turned violent.

Yet the women also had many supporters. The battalion had become a worldwide media sensation, receiving positive attention not only from Russian newspapers but from those of other Allied nations who viewed the women as stellar examples of courage and patriotism. Some Allied journalists even referred to Maria as a Russian Joan of Arc.

One American war correspondent, Bessie Beatty, stayed with the women in their barracks for a week while they awaited their orders to the front. She asked some why they had joined the Battalion of Death. Bessie discovered that many of them had joined because they felt that their country's very existence was at stake and that "nothing but a great human sacrifice could save" it. Some were trying to escape personal issues: "My reasons are so many that I would rather not tell them," one of them told her. Others had lost their entire families in the war: "What else is left for me?" asked one Cossack girl (see sidebar on page 159). Two of the women had been Red Cross nurses and had seen too many Russians die at the hands of the Germans; they felt it would be tragic for Russia to be defeated after so much loss.

After one month of training, the women's battalion received word that it would be sent to the front lines of battle where it was to take part in an important advance into German-controlled territory. The women were deliberately being sent to an area where the male Russian soldiers were on the verge of mutiny.

The night before the advance was to take place, Maria encouraged the women. "Don't be cowards! Don't be traitors," she said. "Remember that you volunteered to set an example to the laggards of the army! I know that you are of the stuff to win glory. The country is watching for you to set an example for the entire front."

Very early the next morning, on July 9, the women soldiers were in the trenches with the 525th Regiment, awaiting the signal to go forward. It came. But the companies on either side of the women, part of the same regiment, didn't move. Instead, the war-weary men argued with their superior officers as the ideal time for charging into battle slipped away.

The women, however, were not at all tired of the war—they were eager to begin, anxious to not disappoint their supporters while proving their detractors wrong.

Finally, a group of 75 officers, accompanied by approximately 300 willing soldiers, approached Maria and asked if they could join the women for an attack. Maria agreed enthusiastically. When the mutineers saw the women and other men preparing to charge, they jeered: "Ha, ha! The women and officers will fight! They are pretending. Who ever saw officers go over the top like soldiers?"

The women cringed but still hoped these jeering men would eventually follow them into battle. When the signal was given, the women and the men with them charged over the top of the trenches, all of them running straight into a hail of German bullets. Through the noise of bombardment the women heard a rumbling behind them. Soon more than half of the corps, those who had initially remained behind, followed them into no-man's-land.

The charge of the 525th Regiment sent the Germans into a retreat, and the Russians were able to secure portions of the Novospasskii Forest. But after reaching the third line of enemy trenches, some of the male Russian soldiers found alcohol left behind by the Germans. They found this treat too tempting to resist. The women tried to break as many bottles as they could, but large numbers of the regiment became drunk, and the advance came to a halt.

The Germans, in the meantime, regrouped and launched a counterattack. The women, along with some of the male soldiers, held their position under six German attacks, but they were not given substantial assistance by any of the nearby units, which forced them to retreat when they finally ran out of ammunition.

The Russians lost all the ground they had gained, and the women suffered the death of three of their company while 36 were wounded. But they captured many surprised German prisoners—"Good God! Women! What a disgrace!"—and proved without a doubt that women could be as battle brave as men. The commander of the 525th Regiment wrote in his official report, "The battalion provided an example of courage, bravery, and composure." Another commander said that "the women's detachment proved that they deserved the name of warrior in the Russian revolutionary army." Ten of the women were awarded the Order of Saint George for courage in action, and 20 others received various other awards.

Bessie Beatty spoke with some of them afterward and asked if they had been afraid. One told her, "We were carried away in the madness of the moment. It was all so strange and exciting, we had no time to think about being afraid." Another said, "No,

I was not afraid. None of us were afraid. We expected to die, so we had nothing to fear."

However much praise the women received for their performance under fire, the men in the armed forces who wanted Russia to pull out of the war highly resented the presence of these inspiring female warriors. When this resentment resulted in violence and death threats, the women of the Battalion of Death had no choice but to disband in mid-December 1917.

Maria then returned to Petrograd, where she refused overtures from the Bolsheviks to join their side. They nearly executed her, but after being rescued by a man who was a former comrade-in-arms, Maria traveled to the United States, where she begged US officials—including President Wilson—to send aid to Russia, which had been in the throes of civil war since the October Revolution. While in the United States, Maria dictated the story of her life to Isaac Don Levine, a Russian writer living in the States. When she returned to Russia, the Bolsheviks eventually arrested her. Following four months of imprisonment and interrogation, Maria was executed on May 16, 1920.

But the admiration for the women in the Battalion of Death had been so great that other groups of military women had sprung up all over Russia, beginning in the spring and summer of 1917, some of them organized officially by the Provisional Government's Ministry of War and some of them run by women's organizations. And following the end of Russia's participation in the Great War, Russian women were utilized in large numbers for combat on both sides of the ensuing Russian Civil War.

LEARN MORE

The Red Heart of Russia by Bessie Beatty (Century Company, 1918) contains a chapter on the Women's Battalion of Death.

They Fought for the Motherland: Russia's Women Soldiers in World War I and the Revolution by Laurie S. Stoff (University of Kansas Press, 2006).

Yashka: My Life as Peasant, Exile and Soldier by Maria Bochkareva with Isaac Don Levine (Constable, 1919).

"Yashka"
Voices of the Great War
www.pbs.org/greatwar/chapters/ch4_voices1.html.

FLORA SANDES

"Remember You're a Soldier"

"Little did I imagine what Fate was hiding up her sleeve for me when the Great War broke out."—Flora Sandes

On the snowy night of November 15, 1916, a British woman in a Serbian army uniform found a spot on the slope of a steep, mountainous incline where she could sleep for the night. The Serbians were in the process of pushing the Bulgarians back from this corner of Serbia, which the Bulgarians had seized a year before. But the Bulgarians still had control of two strongholds, one of them at the top of this peak. The woman was waiting below with the rest of her regiment, approximately 500 men. The regiment had had totaled 2,000 only three months before.

Flora Sandes, c. 1916.
The Flora Sandes Collection

Much had happened in those three months. When she first joined the Serbian army, this woman had seen war as an adventure, the fulfillment of her childhood wish to be involved in a drama similar to that described in one of her favorite poems, "The Charge of the Light Brigade." And as a young woman, she had entertained herself in a most unusual way—taking aim at wild rabbits while on horseback, hoping to one day be part of a dramatic cavalry charge like those she had read about in history books.

Although she would write later that she had taken "to soldiering like a duck to water" and never regretted a moment of her association with the Serbian army, it took only a few weeks for 39-year-old Flora Sandes to realize that war wasn't the grand adventure she had once imagined. It was the drudgery of waiting for hours in cold rain, sleeping in mud, marching over treacherous and rocky hills. It was constant hunger, little water, and the deep sadness of seeing good friends die. Still, Flora loved being a soldier and was determined to face any and all challenges that came her way.

At this moment, as she lay down on the mountainside, she was facing one of her greatest challenges so far: close proximity to the Bulgarians, who, she had been told, tortured their prisoners before executing them.

She and the rest of the regiment, asleep on the cold incline, were suddenly awakened at dawn by the sound of rifle fire and the very audible voices of Bulgarians shouting "Hourra! Hourra!" A group of them were driving a different regiment of Serbs down the mountain. Flora and the men with her charged up to attack whoever had been left to guard the top.

Suddenly, out of the mist, Bulgarians appeared directly in front of Flora and the rest of the regiment. The Bulgarians ducked behind some rocks and threw grenades into the midst of the Serbs. Flora suddenly felt as if a house had fallen on her. She couldn't see. She couldn't get up. She was conscious that the rest of the regiment was retreating.

Lying on that frozen hill, Flora had come a long way from her earlier fantasy that attempting to shoot rabbits would prepare her for actual warfare. And as she had grown older and the rumors of war had grown louder, Flora realized that the only skill that would enable a British woman to participate in war was a thorough knowledge of first aid. So she trained with the First Aid Nursing Yeomanry (FANY) and its "tougher and more practical" offshoot (which Flora had helped create and direct), the Women's Sick and Wounded Convoy Corps.

However, when the war began and she applied to the local Voluntary Aid Detachment (VAD) headquarters, she was turned down. "There are others who are better trained than you," sniffed the woman in charge of hiring. "And anyway," she continued, "the war will only last six months."

But a few days later Flora received a communication that put her in contact with Mabel Grouitch, the American wife of a Serbian official. Mabel had come to England on an urgent mission: she was trying to form a medical unit of surgeons and nurses that could be immediately sent into Serbia to work for the Serbian Red Cross. Determined to be part of the group, Flora was thrilled when Madame Grouitch accepted her. During the trip Flora became close friends with one of the seven other nurses on the team, Emily Simmonds, who had been trained in New York.

After arriving in Serbia at the end of August, the team cared for the wounded in the unventilated, overcrowded, understaffed, and undersupplied First Reserve Military Hospital in Kragujevac, which had been hastily converted from an army barracks. Because the little available anesthetic had to be reserved for the most serious cases, the surgeons often had to operate without it. "The Serbian soldier prides himself on being able to stand an operation," Flora wrote later, commending the Serbs' courage. "They have more endurance than any other race I have ever met."

Flora helped nurse the Serbian soldiers as they successfully repelled two attacks of Austro-Hungarian forces before Flora's three-month contract with the Serbian Red Cross ended. Then she returned to England and raised money—£2,000 in three weeks—for medical supplies that could be taken back to Serbia. Emily had been similarly successful in the United States.

But when they arrived back in Serbia in February 1915, the two women discovered that the country was in the midst of a deadly typhus epidemic. It had begun in the western Serbian city of Valjevo, where many trains and roads intersected. From there the disease had spread throughout much of Serbia. Unsanitary conditions in the country's overflowing POW camps and hospitals, plus the sudden and desperate needs of hundreds of thousands of Serbs who had been made refugees by the Austrian invasion, had quickly sapped all of Serbia's resources, making conditions ripe for an epidemic.

When Colonel Subotić, vice president of the Serbian Red Cross, saw the supplies the women had purchased, he asked if they would consider taking them into Valjevo, still at the heart of the raging epidemic. "I don't like the thought of sending you there," he said, "but your supplies are badly needed as are you." While thinking it over, Flora and Emily discussed their possible plans with an American doctor. He predicted that they would only survive one month, as the current mortality rate in Valjevo was 70 percent.

Ignoring his warning, Flora and Emily arrived in the city on February 20, 1915, where they found thousands of sick men—most of them waiting for treatment in filthy, blood-soaked uniforms—lying everywhere, from the floors of the overflowing hospitals to the streets. Flora and Emily began to work in the largest hospital, where the only doctor still standing greeted them with desperate enthusiasm. The women cleaned, sterilized, and changed bandage dressings and, after watching men die from gangrene on a daily basis because of a surgeon shortage, began to perform their own surprisingly successful operations. They both eventually came down with typhus but recovered due to the skillful help of their orderlies.

Because the typhus epidemic had subsided by the summer of 1915 and because one of the Scottish Women's Hospitals had been established nearby, Flora returned to England. But in October, she learned that Austro-Hungarian forces were attacking Serbia for a third time, now assisted not only by Germany but also by Bulgaria, Serbia's neighbor who had just joined the Central Powers largely because Germany had promised them Serbian territory. Flora quickly made plans to head back, intending to work again for the Serbian Red Cross in Valjevo.

But the Austrian occupation of Valjevo forced Flora to change her plans. Moving from place to place, Flora found that all the hospitals she tried to find work in were being evacuated ahead of the invaders. She realized that the only way she would be allowed to continue to work in Serbia would be by joining one of the medical teams attached to the Serbian army. She joined the nearest one she could find: it was supporting an army regiment and consisted of three covered ox wagons, 12 small tents, and 50 medical personnel. She began a friendship with the regiment's commandant, Colonel Milić who was very impressed with this enthusiastic, fearless English woman who had come to help them.

When the Bulgarians pushed the regiment into an area without roads, making it impossible for the medical team to follow in their ox wagons, it seemed that Flora, too, would have to leave. But staying with the Serbian army was now her dearest wish, so she asked Colonel Milić if she could join the regiment as a soldier with the rank of private.

To her surprise and great delight, he agreed. Then he took her to see the commandant of the entire division, General Miloš Vasić, who warned Flora that the army had immediate plans to retreat through Albania under extremely difficult conditions. In spite of this, he hoped she would stay. Her presence, he said, would encourage the men tremendously; they looked on her as a representative of their ally, England, who they still hoped would one day come to their aid.

So Flora Sandes officially became a private in the Serbian army. The men called her "Nashi Engleskinja" ("Our English-woman"), but soon they stopped thinking of her as a woman at all and called her "brother," the same term they used to address each other.

Writing later, this is what Flora, then with the Fourth Company of the Serbian army, had to say after being involved in her first serious military action against the pursuing Bulgarians:

> It was a most glorious moonlight night, with the ground covered with white hoar frost, and it looked perfectly lovely with all the campfires twinkling every few yards over the hillside among the pine trees. I lay on my back looking up at the stars, and, when one of them asked me what I was thinking about, I told him that when I was old and decrepit and done for, and had to stay in a house and not go about any more, I should remember my first night with the Fourth Company on the top of Mount Chukus.

Then Flora joined the other soldiers—and thousands of other Serbs—in the grueling retreat over the Albanian mountains to

the coast of the Adriatic sea, where they had been promised provisions and help from their allies upon their arrival.

The Great Serbian Retreat

When the Bulgarians joined the Central Powers and
began to invade Serbia's eastern border (while the Germans and Austrians invaded from the west and north),
and as the Allies still hadn't sent the Serbs their promised
help, Serbia's government and military leaders decided
their only option was to evacuate the country. Taking
three main routes, the entire Serbian army, thousands
of Austrian POWs, and thousands of Serbian civilians—
including boys who Serbian military leaders feared would
otherwise be pressed into enemy service—began the
dangerous retreat south and west.

The Serbs had not been able to take much with them
from their war-ravaged country, and the Albanians they
encountered in the mountains were in no mood to help.
Some Serbs had treated them roughly during the Balkan
wars, and most Albanians now saw their chance to retali-
ate, massacring those who could not fight back and bar-
tering unfairly with those who could, taking clothing and
boots from the freezing, starving travelers in exchange
for food.

By the time the survivors reached the Albanian coast
of the Adriatic sea, where they had been promised help
by their allies, approximately 100,000 soldiers and tens
of thousands of civilians had died in the desperate trek.

Flora and the men of the Fourth Company fared better than most during the Great Retreat and reached the coast of Albania on New Year's Eve 1915. Flora became busy with relief efforts—along with her old friend, Emily Simmonds—on behalf of the surviving Serbs. For this, and for saving the lives of many fellow soldiers during the retreat by successfully obtaining food from the Albanians, Flora was promoted from private to sergeant. Then she returned to England where she wrote a book that she hoped would help the Serbians gain British sympathies and support. It was called *An English Woman-Sergeant in the Serbian Army*. Flora was back in Serbia when the book was published that fall.

Partly to test Serbian strength after their ordeal, the Allied command placed the Serbs in charge of removing the Bulgarian strongholds in the Moglena Mountains in the late summer of 1916. While charging up one of the stronghold hills with the Serbian army's Fourth Company of her battalion, Flora was severely wounded by a Bulgarian grenade. Three men of her company dragged her to safety, ignoring Flora's pleas that they not be taken prisoner on her account.

It took the stretcher-bearers two hours to reach the nearest dressing station because they got lost in a blizzard. When they finally arrived and the doctor examined Flora, who was greatly weakened from the cold and loss of blood, he was relieved to find that her wounds, though serious, weren't life-threatening. Her right arm was broken and the flesh in her back and right side was ripped from her shoulder to her knee. Lacking any anesthetic, the doctor began to probe her wound for pieces of shrapnel. When Flora cried out in pain, the doctor said, "Shut up and remember you're a soldier." Flora shut up immediately.

The following day when the Serbs took control of the hill where Flora had been the day before, they found the bodies

SERGEANT-MAJOR FLORA SANDES
THE ONLY BRITISH WOMAN IN THE SERBIAN ARMY

A popular postcard showing Flora Sandes in uniform, 1918. She was by this time a sergeant major and was wearing the Karadjordje Star, the Order of Saint Sava, and the Gold Medal for Bravery.
Flora Sandes Collection

of 10 Serbians lying in a row near the spot where Flora had been hit. Their throats had all been slit.

Reports of the Englishwoman who had been wounded while serving in the Serbian army found their way back to Britain. When Flora returned home to recuperate, she found that she had become a celebrity and a tremendously inspiring figure to many—in a nation where women were not even allowed to vote. Flora used her celebrity status to raise money for the Serbian army, giving speeches in her army uniform and gaining many invitations, even one from Alexandra, the Queen Mother.

Returning to Serbia, Flora rejoined the ranks of the Serbian army during the Serbian advance that drove the Bulgarians, Germans, and Austrians out of Serbia toward the end of the war.

Flora was finally demobilized from the Serbian army in 1922. In 1927 she wrote her second memoir and married Yuri Yudenitch, a former officer of the Imperial Russian Army who had fought with the Russian White Army against the Bolsheviks (who were referred to as the Red Army) during the Russian Civil War. Like many other doomed White Army personnel, he had fled Russia and joined the ranks of the Serbian army during the civil war. During World War II, Flora and Yuri were living in Serbia (which had since become part of Yugoslavia) when Flora was briefly imprisoned by the occupying Germans because she was still a citizen of Britain, one of their enemies.

She died in Suffolk, England, in 1956, at the age of 80.

LEARN MORE

A Fine Brother: The Life of Captain Flora Sandes by Louise Miller (Alma Books, 2012).

The Autobiography of a Woman Soldier: A Brief Record of Adventure with the Serbian Army by Flora Sandes (H. F. and G. Witherby, 1927).

An English Woman-Sergeant in the Serbian Army by Flora Sandes (Hodder and Stoughton, 1916).

MARINA YURLOVA

"I'm a Cossack!"

"Adventure lay just ahead. And the wide world. And war."
—Marina Yurlova, on her way to the war

One evening during the late summer of 1914, Marina Yurlova, a small 14-year-old girl, was eating dinner with her family. Her father, a Cossack who had retired from active military duty and owned large farmlands, told them about the excellent work being done in his fields, all because of a girl: Hanna, the beautiful girlfriend of one of his chief young workers. When she began to work in the fields to be near her boyfriend, she had influenced her crowd of friends to do the same. Hanna was locally famous not only for her beauty but also because of her singing and dancing abilities.

Marina Yurlova.
Cossack Girl *(1936/2010)*

Marina begged her father for permission to join his workers so that she could see this local celebrity for herself. When he reluctantly agreed, Marina rose at 3:00 AM and worked all

Cossacks

The word "Cossack" comes from the Russian *kozak* and Turkish *kazak*, meaning "wanderers" and "free peoples." Cossacks originally descended from a group of Russian peasants who had refused to submit to the virtual slavery enacted by the 16th-century tsars. Instead, they escaped into the area of western Siberia from which they eventually emerged as independent, democratic warrior horsemen. The Cossacks were later required to give several decades of military service to the tsars, who used them as a buffer against Russia's enemies. In return the Cossacks were given large portions of land. At least half of Russia's cavalry during the First World War were Cossacks, and they were one of Russia's most quickly mobilized groups when the war began.

Cossacks during World War I.
Great War Document Archive, 1461

morning with the rest of the young people. When they stopped for lunch, Hanna began to dance and sing for them. Suddenly the loud clanging of church bells interrupted her performance. Galloping horses brought Cossacks rushing into the field. "War! War!" they cried.

The young men in the group immediately followed the other Cossacks to the next town square, with the women following behind, including Marina. When they arrived in the square, where news of the war's outbreak was being announced, everyone there began to shout, "To arms! To arms! For tsar and country!" When the young women decided to follow the men to the train stations, Marina, swept up in the excitement, followed them even when the women boarded the train, hoping to follow the men as far as they would be allowed.

A soldier came through the train cars, asking for everyone's name.

"Who are you, little girl?" he asked Marina. "Where is your father?"

Marina's father was well known in military circles; identifying herself as his daughter would have quickly ended her exciting journey. She gave him a false surname and a lie, telling him that her father was in the troop train just ahead.

Day after day went by as the train took Marina farther and farther away from her home. Writing later, she said, "It was too late to turn back, nor would I have done so if I could. Adventure lay just ahead. And the wide world. And war."

When the women came to the final stop, they wandered around different military camps for days until they found the men from their group. Marina, who obviously wasn't expecting to find anyone she knew, suddenly found herself alone, terribly afraid, and in tears. She was rescued by a kind Cossack sergeant named Koskoff. Called Kosel by his men, he took pity on the young girl. Marina continued to lie about trying to find her father, and Kosel promised to help her find him.

In the meantime, since her work dress had become very worn, Kosel sent Marina to his brother, a maker of Cossack uniforms, to get a uniform of her own. Wearing her new uniform gave Marina confidence and made her stand out less. She immediately began to make herself useful by taking care of the regiment horses, an activity she felt very comfortable with. Because she was such a hard worker, the rest of the regiment eventually gave her grudging respect.

After several months, the regiment was moved to the Caucasus region, an area where both the Ottoman and Russian empires had sent their troops to battle over certain territories.

Marina accompanied the men one night as they went out of the camp to gather information on their surroundings. The men handed their horses' reins to Marina and walked silently away. Marina was terrified. She was certain that an enemy soldier would approach her in the silent darkness and slit her throat. But nothing happened. On the way back, when Kosel asked her, "Well, Marina, what did you think of sentry duty?" she lied, glad that the darkness was hiding her face: "It's not bad. But it does seem rather dull."

Kosel must have believed her because later that night, at two in the morning, someone woke her for a different type of sentry duty inside the camp. Marina was thrilled: she knew that this was an important responsibility. All she had to do was stay awake at her post. After a while doing just that became quite painful, but she managed. In the morning, Kosel congratulated her on being a good soldier.

One day, Marina was out exploring the area with Kosel and some others of their regiment among the foothills of the Caucasus mountains. Suddenly, as they came from around a hill, they

The Caucasus Front

When Germany convinced the Turk-run Ottoman Empire to attack the Russian Empire in mountainous Russian Caucasia, it opened up an entirely new front of war. Russia was now forced to divert some of its military from the eastern front, which was exactly what Germany had intended. (Russia's allies, in an attempt to divert the Turks away from Caucasia, decided to attack the Turkish forts at Gallipoli.) The Turks wanted to regain territories in the Caucasus that had been taken from them by the Russians during the Russo-Turkish War of 1877–78, some of which was inhabited by their fellow Muslims. Key in this struggle were the Armenians, a largely Christian group—some of whom lived on one side of the border between the empires, some on the other—who were developing their own sense of nationalism. There were Armenian men in the armies of both empires, a fact that would have tragic consequences as the war on the Caucasus front developed.

caught sight of a huge camp of Turks across the Araks River. They seemed to Marina like a "great black sea of men." It was the first time any of them had seen the enemy.

After Kosel reported the situation back to his *sotnik* (his superior officer), the Cossack officers stayed up all night in conference. Before the sun came up, the *sotnik* came out with the general, who addressed the part of the regiment that was awake. He told them that they didn't have enough men or ammunition to hold back the enemy, but if they didn't try to do something immediately, the Turks would soon reach the main railroad that led straight into the heart of Russia. Someone needed to destroy the bridges across the Araks River to at least slow the enemy's advance. "Russia is asking a sacrifice of you," he said. "Who will volunteer to die for our mother Russia and our father tsar?"

Marina saw the tears in his eyes and those of the men he was addressing. She watched to see who would step up first. No one moved. Suddenly she felt her own legs stepping forward. Before she knew what was happening, she was standing in front of the general, her hand raised in a salute.

"You?" he replied. "You're only a child!"

"I'm a Cossack!" Marina replied.

Kosel rushed to Marina's side. "Child," he said, "you don't know what you're doing—fighting is for men." Marina could hear movement behind them. Twelve men had also come forward. Kosel asked the general if that number would be enough. "Take the 12," the general replied, and then, smiling and saluting Marina, he added, "and also this Cossack."

It was still dark when they set out for the bridges. They set fire to two wooden bridges. But as they made preparations to blow up the third and largest, a bridge made of concrete, dawn was breaking. Machine-gun fire suddenly began to fly in their direction. They must been spotted by the Turks. Kosel told Marina to stay down as he went a little ahead to touch off the fuse. He was hit. Marina saw him die, blood spurting from his forehead. A great explosion followed. The concrete bridge was destroyed.

Marina, hit in the leg by a bullet and overcome with sorrow at the loss of her best friend, was the only one of the 13 to survive the attack on the bridges.

By midsummer 1915, Marina's *sotnik* told her that their general had recommended her for a Cross of Saint George medal, the Russian army's highest military award for exceptional courage. When Kurny, another superior officer, brought it over to her while she was eating dinner with others from their regiment, there was a dead silence.

"What's eating you all?" Kurny demanded angrily.

"*She* didn't blow up the bridge," one man grumbled. The others muttered in agreement.

"Shut up, you," barked Kurny. "She didn't blow up the bridge, but she was the first one to volunteer, and the only one left of them all."

But Marina had to agree: she didn't feel that she deserved the award either.

In the autumn of 1915, the Russian army on the Caucasus front had plenty of ammunition but no skirmishes and little food. There was so little food in the area that some of the starving Armenians who had been with the Russians tried to go over to the Turks to get food. Marina and the other men saw one of these soldiers as he attempted to return, crawling on the ground, caked with blood and mud. One eye was gone, one hand was gone, and his tongue was slit. Marina suddenly became sick. All the others, except Kurny, laughed at her. Marina was also confronted with bands of starving, begging Armenian children who roamed the countryside.

In January 1916, the Russian army in the Caucasus was preparing for a major attack. As Marina watched thousands of men from all over Russia marching through the freezing cold, gathering for battle against Erzurum, a large city in eastern Turkey (and the Ottoman base of operations in the area), she wasn't filled with the patriotism that had once made her proud to be part of a Cossack regiment.

The new conscripts, who looked miserable with their vacant stares and hunched shoulders, had been given only a few days

The Armenian Genocide

"Here there was no question of taking necessary measures for protection or defense. This was murder for the sheer joy of it, the deliberate extermination of an entire nation."

—*Claire Studer Goll, German writer protesting official German apathy in light of the Armenian genocide*

There had long been extremists within the Ottoman Empire's ruling government, the Young Turks, who claimed that the only way to strengthen the declining empire was to purge it of non-Muslim peoples. The Armenians—the empire's largest group of Christians—had been officially and savagely persecuted by the Turks for decades. When the presence of Armenian soldiers within the Russian army was publicly and falsely blamed for Turkish military defeats at the hands of the Russians during the war's first year, Armenian soldiers in the Ottoman army were taken out of active duty, and a plan to destroy all Armenians became official Turkish policy. Approximately one million Armenian men, women, and children were tortured, maimed, and killed. To this day, the Turkish government refuses to use the term "genocide" when discussing this mass slaughter.

of training before being forced onto a train. When Marina overheard one officer complaining to another that there was nowhere to put them, the second officer revealed their ultimate purpose: they were to be marched out first, straight into enemy fire. "Keep a heavy guard over them until we go into action," he said. "They'll be the first meat."

As both sides launched deadly artillery attacks on each other, Marina carried dispatches (important official communications) between the front lines and field headquarters. One day she handed a dispatch to an officer at headquarters. As she waited for his reply she heard him tell the other officers that he was ordering a new advance, one that would cost many lives. As she rode back to the front with the dispatch, Marina knew that she was carrying a message of death. She felt that she, not the officer, was sending these soldiers to their deaths. She longed to destroy the order and ride away. Instead, she decided to delay the advance ever so slightly by taking the long way back to the front.

When the dispatch was delivered, Marina could see its results immediately. She heard the orders to advance being shouted everywhere. She and other Cossacks marched behind the initial advance. Their orders were to check the artillery gun emplacements and also dig holes in which the next wave of infantry could find temporary shelter from the enemy's artillery.

Making their way through the bodies of the dead and wounded that littered the field, they found a spot, and Marina began to dig, soon exhausted by the work and counting in order to stay awake: *One, two, three* . . . By the time she got to seven, she had been knocked unconscious.

She awoke to the sound of distant guns. She couldn't move. She was lying half-buried in the dirt. She could see the bright red sunset and a few stars in the sky. She could hear wild dogs in the distance, their barking coming closer and closer.

But some Russians, searching for survivors, found Marina in time and brought her to a hospital in Tiflis (now Tbilisi), the capital city of Georgia, where she woke up a few days later in the officers' ward. She was told that she'd suffered a concussion, most likely the result of a shell. She received another Cross of Saint George medal for, in her words, "being buried . . . I suppose."

After two months of hospitalization, Marina received automobile training and worked for the army as a driver. While she was transporting the wounded, the enemy began shelling the hospital transport trucks behind the lines. Marina's truck was hit, and she suffered a second concussion.

Marina's second concussion resulted in a neurological condition that caused her head to swing back and forth continuously. While she was recuperating, someone told Marina about the February Revolution: Russia no longer had a tsar. Marina immediately thought of Kosel, realizing that he "had died for a cause that did not exist any more, that had been overthrown in a night. . . . Kosel, and my comrades, and a million others."

The Tsar and the Russian National Identity

Although on the one hand the autocratic tsarist state was generally considered oppressive, many Russians also regarded the tsar as a powerful, mystical, and religious symbol of their nation. When Tsar Nicholas II's reign came to an end—and with it the 300-year Romanov dynasty—many Russians celebrated, believing (falsely, it turned out) that they would now experience the freedoms of democracy. But many others felt a sense of disorientation and loss.

In September 1918, she and the other less seriously injured patients were moved to Kazan, a city on the Volga River that was now in the control of the Bolsheviks.

One day, Bolsheviks posted in all the hospital wards lists of those wounded soldiers they thought were sufficiently recovered to begin training for the Bolshevik army. Marina was among those on the list; she and the rest of these recruits were ordered to report to the Kazan university. Upon arrival, they were immediately asked by a Bolshevik student what side they belonged to, which government they believed in.

Marina, not quite ready for the question, said that she "believed in any government that protected our Mother Russia and stood for her honor." She was immediately confronted by another young Bolshevik who condemned her for being a Cossack, a killer of Jews, and an oppressor of workers and peasants. Marina tried to defend herself against his accusations, blurting out, "Brothers, I fought with you and for you since the first year of the war, for the love of country and religion." Then, either from exhaustion or fear, she fainted. When she woke up she found herself in prison.

But she was soon rescued by Czechoslovakian prisoners of war who had escaped and joined forces with the White Army troops against the Bolsheviks and who had just driven the Bolsheviks out of Kazan. Marina, free to make her own choice, chose to join them against the Bolsheviks. She was wounded, sent back to Kazan, and then forced to evacuate when the Bolsheviks retook the town.

Managing to avoid them, Marina finally arrived at an American-run hospital in the port city of Vladivostok where, after a stay of three weeks, she was given a passport and means of passage to Japan. She later moved to the United States and wrote her memoirs in 1936 and 1937.

LEARN MORE

Cossack Girl by Marina Yurlova (Macaulay Company, 1936; reprinted by Heliograph, 2010).

The Only Woman by Marina Yurlova (Macaulay Company, 1937).

ECATERINA TEODOROIU

Lieutenant Girl

"She seemed a warrior child, with her pale face, with her ardent eyes, with her short-cut hair."
—Romanian Colonel Lieutenant N. Teodorescu,
speaking of Ecaterina Teodoroiu

On the morning of October 14, 1916, two German troops were just north of the Romanian city of Târgu Jiu. The Romanian army had initiated hostilities with the Central Powers when, just months earlier in August, they had invaded Transylvania, part of the Austria-Hungarian empire but also home to millions of Romanians who had long been persecuted by the Hungarians. The Austrians and Hungarians and their allies, the Germans

Ecaterina Teodoroiu in uniform.
National Military Museum, Romania

(who had more soldiers and weapons than the Romanians), had pushed back hard and were now inside Romania's borders.

At nine o'clock that morning, the Germans had reached the bridge over the Jiu River that led into Târgu Jiu. There were only 150 Romanian soldiers in the local garrison, not nearly enough to repel the Germans. Reinforcements were promised, but time was running out. The Germans were getting closer.

Suddenly, civilians from Târgu Jiu appeared: old men, women, and children eager to defend their city, carrying whatever weapons they could find. "To Jiu! To the bridge!" they cried. "We must defend the bridge! We will not let the enemy enter our town!"

Many who witnessed the fierce civilian defense of the bridge that day were especially impressed with the city's women and girls, who, despite the obvious danger, fired weapons, transported ammunition, and tended the wounded. One eyewitness noticed in particular a young woman who was guiding some Romanian troops to the bridge. Then she joined the other scouts—her orders and encouragements heard amid the roar of the guns—who were taking an enthusiastic and active role in the defense of the bridge, firing weapons on the enemy.

The young woman's name was Ecaterina Teodoroiu. Her parents had given her the name Cătălina when she was born in 1894 in the Romanian village of Văleni near Târgu Jiu.

Because she was such an excellent student, her parents had encouraged her to continue her education past the grade-school level—not something that Văleni villagers normally did. She enrolled at a boarding school in Bucharest, Romania's capital city, where she had won a scholarship contest. She was initially behind in certain subjects, foreign languages especially, and her wealthy fellow students excluded and insulted her, calling her a "peasant."

Yet she was a determined student, and her teachers—who changed her name from Cătălina to Ecaterina—were amazed at her progress. She wanted to become a teacher who would return home and teach the village children about Romania. In order to prepare for this, she studied history intensely, which in turn gave her a great pride in her Romanian heritage. Her growing patriotism also inspired her in 1913 to become involved in a local scout troop, a serious activity for patriotic young Romanians. Ecaterina became part of the first female Romanian scout troop in Bucharest.

After finishing her courses at the boarding school but before initiating the additional schooling for her teacher's certificate, Ecaterina returned to Văleni, where she became active in another group of scouts located in the nearby town of Târgu Jiu. The group was called "Mr. Tudor," named for Tudor Vladimirescu, a Romanian military hero who in the early 19th century had fought for the independence of his people. Ecaterina eventually became Mr. Tudor's leader.

Then during the summer of 1916, Romania became part of the world war. The country's motivation for getting involved was a desire for the creation of a "Greater Romania," the joining together of all ethnic Romanians into a single kingdom. Since that would involve annexing lands currently belonging to the Austro-Hungarian empire, Romania joined the nations of the Allies, who promised them the lands of Transylvania and Bukovina (among several others) upon victory.

On August 28, 1916, when King Ferdinand proclaimed to the Romanian people that they were at war with the Central Powers, he said that going to war would "complete the task of our forefathers . . . to establish forever that which Michael the Great was only able to establish for a moment, namely, a Rumanian union."

Two Years of Romanian Neutrality

Why did Romania remain neutral for so long? Although King Ferdinand of Romania wanted territory belonging to Austria-Hungary, and although Allied diplomats promised him these lands if he would join their side, the king felt a strong degree of loyalty to the Central Powers. He was German-born and was related to both the tsar of Bulgaria and the emperor of Austria-Hungary. His uncle and predecessor, Carol I of Romania, had even, years earlier, pledged Romania to the Central Powers. And the Allied nations would be allies in name only: Great Britain and France were far away and Russia, while much closer, would be somewhat indifferent; it wanted some of the same territory Romania did. Romania's army was poorly trained and dangerously short of equipment; Romania had no munitions factories and had previously imported most of its military supplies from Germany and Austria, who both immediately stopped sending them when the war began. Yet, after two years of negotiations, impatient Allied diplomats were finally able to convince Romania that the summer of 1916 was the right moment to join their side.

Ecaterina's brothers immediately joined the army. To do her part, Ecaterina—as part of the Mr. Tudor scout troop—decided to work as a volunteer nurse at a medical station close to the fighting, near the Jiu River. She and the other scouts from Mr. Tudor took an active military role on October 16, 1916, when the Germans tried to cross the bridge over the Jiu River and the local civilians successfully repelled them. Afterward, Ecaterina decided to work closer to the lines of fighting, where she often came under direct fire.

One cold day in October, General Ion Dragalina stopped his car to speak with the wounded on a battlefield near where Ecaterina was working. He saw Ecaterina and asked her why she was placing herself in such danger. She answered, "The country is in danger. My heart wouldn't let me to stay apart."

Impressed, General Dragalina placed his own fur coat over her shoulders, saying, "Well done, my child. You are a true heroine."

The enemy continued to push the Romanian army back, farther and farther. This made Ecaterina want to take a more active role in Romania's defense. Her desire became even more intense when she learned that her brother Ion had been killed in battle.

She decided to fight beside her brother Nicolae, who was now a sergeant-instructor. Though not officially part of the regiment Nicolae belonged to, Ecaterina was accepted by them all as a fellow soldier. One of the regiment officers, Major Liviu Teieseanu, later said that during this time Ecaterina was a "true example for the soldiers," patiently enduring with them "the brunt of war" and participating in all their actions, even dangerous bayonet charges.

One day, Ecaterina—just a little ways off from her brother—heard the whistle of a shell coming closer and closer. It fell near Nicolae and killed him.

Wanting to avenge her brother's death, Ecaterina requested permission to serve in his place. Romanian women weren't normally allowed to be an official (or unofficial, for that matter) part of the military, but understanding the sincere and intense motive behind Ecaterina's request, the military leaders agreed.

On November 4, 1916, the soldiers from Ecaterina's regiment defending the south side of Târgu Jiu were outnumbered and nearly surrounded by the Germans, who requested that they surrender and become prisoners. When the Germans approached, Ecaterina stepped forward out of the lines and explained, in German, that the regiment had decided to surrender. Then she suddenly began shooting, killing several Germans. In the confusion that followed, most of the company was able to escape while Ecaterina and several other soldiers were captured.

But while she was being led away by a German sentry, Ecaterina took advantage of a moment of his inattention and shot him with a gun she had hidden in her uniform. As she and the other Romanians ran off into the darkness, a German soldier, hearing the noise, shot in her direction, wounding her in her right leg. In spite of the pain she was able to return to her military company the same night, to everyone's astonishment.

Shortly after this, an exploding shell seriously wounded both of Ecaterina's legs. While recuperating in the hospital, she was awarded the rank of second lieutenant, becoming the first female officer in the Romanian army.

By the spring of 1917, enormous sections of Romania were overrun by the Germans and Austrians. Not only did the dream of a Greater Romania seem forever lost but the war had caused great suffering among Romanian civilians: grieving widows and starving orphans wandered the roads in search of food. All of this suffering made Ecaterina more determined than ever to continue the fight.

After being discharged from the hospital, she joined a new regiment that was in the midst of a typhoid epidemic. Relying on her previous nursing experience, Ecaterina took charge of disinfecting procedures that helped stop the epidemic. She was awarded the Scouting Virtue gold medal for her efforts along with the Military Virtue medal for her previous courage in battle.

During the spring of 1917, the Romanian military leadership, assisted by the French, took serious steps to reorganize and retrain its remaining forces. Ecaterina took advantage of all the training available to her, eager to prove herself worthy of her new rank. Now the commander of a troop, she was given the authority to instruct other soldiers, often substituting for her own commander when he wasn't available to teach.

The Romanian army emerged from its period of reorganization ready to fight more effectively. Their subsequent victory during the Battle of Mărăşti greatly surprised the Germans and Austrians and gave the Romanian army a new sense of confidence as they prepared for another battle, one that would be fought at Mărăşeşti.

As the units in Ecaterina's division—kept in reserve until the final days of the battle—marched toward Mărăşeşti, they were impatient to face the enemy. One of the commanders spoke with Ecaterina as she marched along with her troop, asking her if she had enough food for herself in the provisions bag she was carrying.

Ecaterina answered that yes, she had food—but it was not for herself; it was for the Germans. She showed him her bag: it was full of bullets.

But when her troop arrived near the battlefields of Mărăşeşti, she was advised to stay in the trenches. Her division commander knew how dangerous the battle would be and didn't want Ecaterina to be killed. He ordered her instead to tend the wounded. Ecaterina protested. "If you care about me," she pleaded, "please don't advise me to do a deed that later will bring shame on me and on you."

Her commander relented.

And so Ecaterina found herself exactly where she wanted to be: waiting for the signal to advance with the rest of her troop. The German artillery began to pound the Romanian line. Then the German infantry advanced, and the Romanians went out to meet them. Bullets flew. Cannons thundered. Groans could be heard everywhere.

The members of Ecaterina's unit, attempting to take an area close to the German line, advanced more quickly than the other units around them, leaving them somewhat unprotected. Ecaterina, in the front, shouted, "Move forward, boys! Don't give up! You are with me!"

The next moment she was hit in the chest by German bullets, dying almost immediately. All day and late into the night, news of her death spread among the soldiers with these words: "The second lieutenant girl has died! The second lieutenant girl has died!"

The Romanian army won the Battle of Mărăşeşti, despite the fact that the war-weary and Bolshevik-influenced Russian soldiers who were supposed to be fighting alongside them had largely retreated without a struggle when the enemy approached.

When the Russian army began to fully disintegrate and prey on Romanian civilians, Romania, surrounded by enemies, had no hope of initiating—or winning—another battle. They were forced to sign an armistice with the Central Powers on December 9, 1917.

But after enduring a humiliating and brutal German occupation for nearly a year, Romania rejoined the Allies on November 10, 1918, one day before the general armistice. After the war Queen Marie of Romania pressured the Allied nations to keep their prewar promises to expand Romania's borders, helping assure the creation of a Greater Romania, the nation's original aim for entering the war.

Queen Marie of Romania

"I should die of grief if Romania were to go to war against England."

—*Queen Marie of Romania*

Just as her husband, King Ferdinand, with his German background, found it difficult to join the Allies, so too did Queen Marie—closely related to the royal houses of both England and Russia (and possessed of a more forceful personality than her husband)—find it impossible to consider Romania joining the Central Powers. Granddaughter to both Queen Victoria and Tsar Alexander II of Russia, Marie was adored by the citizens of her adopted country for many reasons, the most important being that she made Romania's war aims her own. After spending much of the war raising money for the Red Cross and visiting wounded soldiers, in 1919 Marie traveled to the Paris Peace Conference when it became clear that the Allied leaders there had lost interest in honoring their prewar agreements to Romania. Creating a media sensation (as she had hoped), she managed to pressure the Allied leaders into giving Romania the lands of Romanian-speaking peoples.

Queen Marie of Romania.
Library of Congress, LC-DIG-ggbain-17546

Ecaterina Teodoroiu was now more than just a battle hero: she was regarded as someone who had given her life in the struggle for Greater Romania. Those who had personally known her worked to keep her memory alive. Testimonies, documents, and objects relating to her life and service were collected and eventually placed in several locations, such as her childhood home (which later became a museum) and in a room of the Central Military Museum in Bucharest.

In 1921 her body was exhumed from the place it had been buried near the spot where she had fallen, placed in a coffin made from the steel of German cannons, and reburied in a state funeral run by military and civic leaders and attended by enormous crowds. Multiple monuments bearing her likeness were erected in her honor, streets were named after her, and poems and plays were written about her. The second lieutenant girl had become a national hero.

LEARN MORE

The Last Romantic: The Life of the Legendary Marie, Queen of Roumania by Hannah Pakula (Simon and Schuster, 1984) is a clear history of Romania and its royal family during the war.

The Romanian Battlefront in World War I by Glenn E. Torrey (University Press of Kansas, 2011).

PART IV

JOURNALISTS

"Under certain conditions newspapers rule the fate of nations; events in this war reveal this as an incontrovertible fact."

—Dorothy Lawrence, British woman who posed
as a man to report on the western front

There are many firsthand accounts of World War I from people who witnessed it. Many observers and participants published their memoirs immediately after the war while others did so during the 1930s when it became clear that the world was gearing up for another global conflict.

But there were other writers, many of them sent by news agencies and newspapers, who tried to report on the war as it was happening. They had one problem: their governments' careful control of the news.

News organizations in the combatant countries didn't have to work hard to convince their readers to support the war when it first began: journalists on all sides of the conflict had been creating enormously negative images of the enemy in the minds of their readers for decades.

But would these perceptions remain strong enough to inspire civilian support of the war to its end? The governments of the combatant nations apparently didn't think so: their presses immediately went to work for the war effort and most journalists were ready and willing to cooperate with their governments' requests for war-related propaganda.

"The few papers that arrived were so severely censored that, apart from wildly exaggerated accounts of Belgian victories, we knew nothing of events."

—Princess Marie de Croÿ, Belgian resister,
at the beginning of the war

However, the war most people had imagined, which had inspired such overwhelming initial enthusiasm was very different from the war that actually occurred. Some of the high-ranking military leaders who were responsible for giving orders that wasted young lives by the thousands would not even come near the front lines of battle: they knew if they saw the results of their orders they might stop giving them.

If these leaders weren't willing to see firsthand the result of their own plans, they certainly didn't want the public to have access to that information. The people on the home front were being asked to do with less whenever possible so that the armies at the front would have enough food and materials with which to wage war.

"Whatever is printed in German newspapers is the truth as far as it goes, but not everything that is known is printed. What the people really get is the truth without the details."

—Mary McAuley, American in wartime Germany

As the war dragged on and the lists of those killed in battle—one of the few true items regularly printed in the papers—became longer and longer, and reporters became ever more curious, the governments of the main combatant countries took increasingly drastic measures to suppress the truth. Letters written home by soldiers were carefully censored, as were the "trench journalism" newspapers that were written and edited by and for the fighting men on both sides of the western front. Journalists who were near the front, trying to get a scoop for the readers at home, were kept under close supervision, and what they printed was heavily censored.

In this environment of carefully controlled information, where male journalists were barely tolerated by the military near the front lines, fully qualified female journalists were often rejected completely. While some of these women eventually succeeded in touring hospitals and trenches under close supervision—usually without being officially accredited by military authorities, which meant that they were excluded from official military briefings and had to find their own places to stay— some women decided to break through these barriers by taking on roles that would grant them inside access to a story.

For instance, Dorothy Lawrence, a 19-year-old British woman, traveled to France at the war's outbreak in order to get an inside story by posing as a man in the British Expeditionary Force (BEF). She found work as a sapper (digging tunnels) on the western front. But when she became sick, she decided that turning herself in (instead of having her gender discovered while being treated) might help prevent the punishment of the men who had helped her deceive her superiors.

She was immediately arrested, interrogated repeatedly by a large number of British officers, and accused of being a spy—and then a prostitute. When finally released, Dorothy was forbidden to leave France or write about her experiences. After the war, when she was finally free to write and publish her book, *Sapper Dorothy Lawrence*, it was highly censored by the British Ministry of Defence and not fully published until decades later when it was accidentally discovered.

Another woman whose unique attempt at getting a story eventually produced a book was American writer Ellen LaMotte. Frustrated by the difficulties put in the way of female journalists, LaMotte decided that working as a nurse in a French hospital in Belgium would give her the story she was looking for. The resulting book, *The Backwash of War*, was published in 1916 and contained nothing of the glory and heroism that most of the combatant countries were attempting to promote. Instead, LaMotte's book detailed the agonizing last hours of men who, although medically attended to, often died without being near anyone who knew or loved them. *The Backwash of War* was immediately banned by the governments of France and Great Britain but sold well in the United States until that country joined the war—then LaMotte's book was banned there, as well.

LaMotte's was not the only wartime book banned by the United States government. While Madeleine Zabriskie Doty's book, *Short Rations*—which described life on the German home front and was published before America's entry into the war—was fairly well received in the United States, another similar book wasn't. *Germany in War Time*, published after America's entrance into the war and written by American Mary McAuley, was considered far too sympathetic toward ordinary Germans. Upon its publication, *Germany in War Time* was immediately seized by the US government.

Although the western front was probably the most difficult place for a female journalist to get a story, there was an exception: the unoccupied section of Belgium, where leaders were desperate to fight German propaganda regarding the brutal invasion of Belgium (see sidebar on page 192). And on the eastern front, during the final months of Russia's participation in the war, the Provisional Government, which had deposed the tsar and was desperately trying to keep Russia in the war, gladly welcomed curious reporters from all over the world who had come to see the Women's Battalion of Death. Some of these reporters—men and women—also braved the turmoil of the subsequent Bolshevik Revolution that plunged Russia into years of civil war.

MARY ROBERTS RINEHART

Mystery Writer on the Western Front

"I am to go to the firing line. No woman has gone there yet."

—*Mary Roberts Rinehart*

When the Germans invaded Belgium in August 1914, it caused Mary Roberts Rinehart some sleepless nights. Her insomnia had nothing to do with concern for the Belgians, though; she couldn't yet grasp what was happening to them. And she wasn't worried about her three sons being sent

Mary Roberts Rinehart in 1915 when she went to Europe.
Mary Roberts Rinehart Papers, 1831–1970, SC.1958.03, Special Collections Department, University of Pittsburgh

overseas; they weren't yet old enough to serve in the military, and anyway, America was neutral. Her insomnia was caused by her own burning desire to see the war. "I had at that time," she wrote later, "no hatred of war, only a great interest and a great curiosity. . . . I imagine that my feeling was much that of the average man who enlists. Later he may lay his act to duty, to patriotism, to the furtherance of some great cause. But very often he enlists for the adventure."

In the early 20th century it was a highly unusual step for a married woman with children to consider leaving her family temporarily for a dangerous war zone, but Mary's success as a mystery author had already made her life as a wife and mother somewhat unusual. Most upper-class American women in 1914 did not have incomes separate from their husbands', but Mary's writing had made her wealthy. She was also a regular contributor to the *Saturday Evening Post*, an enormously popular American weekly magazine that published fiction, news, and editorials. The *Post's* editor, George Horace Lorimer, had already sent two correspondents to Europe, but when he received Mary's request to be sent specifically into Belgium, he agreed, knowing that anything she wrote would sell more magazines. He was a bit nervous about sending the mother of young children into a country that was at war, but he understood "the appeal that [war] makes to every writer, man or woman," adding that he was "tempted to throw up my job and go myself."

Mary arrived in London in January 1915. Lorimer had given her a letter of introduction to Lord Northcliffe, a powerful and influential British news publisher. When she told him she wanted to travel to the front lines of the war, he told her that would be impossible—hundreds of international journalists were stuck in London because they were vainly attempting to do the same thing.

But within a week Mary was sailing out of London and toward Belgium. She had convinced the Anglo-Belgian committee of the Belgian Red Cross, headquartered in London, that her nurses' training, obtained when she was a young woman, made her exceptionally qualified to report on the conditions of the Belgian army hospitals and how well the American hospital supplies were being distributed there. "Let me see conditions as they really are," she pleaded. They replied with a question: "Where do you wish to go?"

What would her answer be? Seeing the Belgian army hospitals was only part of what Mary wanted to do. She wanted to see for herself how the new means of warfare affected ordinary Belgian soldiers. She wanted to meet the ones who were still fighting in the small section of unoccupied Belgium. What were these men thinking? How did they live? How did they die? The newspapers printed only vague information, "details that meant nothing" to Mary.

So her answer to the Belgian Red Cross leaders was that she wanted to go "everywhere." They gave her letters of introduction addressed to leaders in the Belgian army and then something that no other journalist waiting in London had: a special residency card that would enable Mary to easily exit Britain for Belgium, where she could stay indefinitely and see the front lines (unlike other journalists, who, if they gained access to the Belgian front, would be allowed only a 24-hour stay).

Mary toured Belgian hospitals where she became "obsessed by the injustice, the wanton waste and cost" of human lives, both civilian and soldier. When she visited the trenches and saw (and smelled) how the men were forced to live in those small, filthy, wet areas, she began to feel anger toward the Germans, whose invasion had forced the Belgians there. She watched helplessly as homes behind the Belgian trenches (but within range of

German artillery) were destroyed, sometimes killing civilians who were attempting to survive in their bombed-out villages.

After Mary had been in Belgium for three weeks she was told that she had been included in a small group of international journalists who would be allowed a tour of the Belgian front, including a trip into no-man's-land, the first time this had been allowed for any correspondents.

She and the other journalists met the commanding officers at the Belgian army headquarters, often passing long lines of soldiers who stood silently in the rain to let their cars go by. "That is the thing that impressed me always about the lines of soldiers I saw going to and from the trenches," she wrote later, "their silence." Mary and the other journalists drove down a road that ran parallel to the advance trenches (the line of trenches closest to no-man's-land). In the night sky, Mary could see the magnesium flares (called *fusées* in French) sent into the sky by the Germans—sometimes 12 at once—that silently but clearly illuminated everything within sight for about 60 seconds.

After continuing this journey behind the advance trenches on foot, Mary asked a Belgian captain to explain why the Belgians had flooded no-man's-land two to eight feet deep with seawater as a successful defense against the Germans. He told Mary that the surface of the water hid not only holes and ditches that attacking Germans would trip over but also that barbed wire was hidden beneath the surface. The water contained many dead bodies that couldn't be retrieved. "The odour of that beautiful lagoon was horrible," Mary wrote. "Any lingering belief that I may have had in the grandeur and glory of war died that night beside that silver lake—died of an odour."

After passing an area where there had been extremely heavy fighting and where a major was now posted, flat on his stomach, with a machine gun pointed toward the German lines, the journalists and their hosts came to the most dangerous part of the trip. They were to walk straight out into no-man's-land upon a slippery four-foot-wide path made of sandbags, covered with twigs, that rose out of the midst of the water. Their destination was the "shaking, rocking" tower of a ruined church, now being used as a Belgian observation post, 400 yards from the Belgian front lines and only 600 feet away from the Germans. The journalists had been given only one warning: "If a *fusée* goes up, stand perfectly still. If you move they will fire." But the Germans wouldn't need a *fusée* to see them that night; the moon was very bright. Mary suddenly regretted her decision to wear a khaki-colored coat. "I shone like a star," she recorded in her diary. She felt that "a thousand rifles" were "picking her out."

After a moment's fearful hesitation Mary stepped out onto the pathway and walked out to the tower. After climbing the rope ladder, she met the individual manning the tower: a Belgian officer-turned-monk who had returned to the military when the war had begun and who was using his post to report important observations via a telephone. Mary was so close to the German lines at this point that she could see the individual sandbags of the front trench. "No more gallant act than his can be imagined," Mary wrote in her diary, describing the man in the tower. "He waits alone, telephone in hand, the ruined tower rocking. . . . Shells fly about him. He is the constant target of the trenches. But he climbs his ladder. . . . It is for Belgium." Mary wished him good luck and returned along the pathway.

No *fusées* had gone up, and there was no firing on them from the German line—only one close call from a young, surprised Belgian sentry who didn't initially recognize the journalists on their way back and who took aim at them before he was stopped. Mary later discovered that the Belgian officer in charge of the entire expedition had had no intention of allowing a woman to walk into no-man's-land and that when he saw her from a distance beginning the trek, he was furious but powerless to stop her; calling out would have alerted the Germans.

A few days later Mary had an adventure of a very different nature: her request for a personal interview with the king of Belgium had been granted. King Albert had become an internationally inspiring symbol of resistance when he had convinced his government to refuse the powerful German war machine peaceful passage through Belgium. King Albert and Queen Elizabeth lived in La Panne, a coastal town in the small section of unoccupied Belgium where the queen had established a Red Cross hospital.

Mary, wanting to assist Belgium in some way, hoped to get an official statement from the king directed to America. After receiving formal instruction on royal protocol, Mary was ushered into his presence at Belgian army headquarters. "I advanced," she wrote later, "and a very tall man standing on the hearth rug came forward gravely and held out his hand. I shook it fervently, and waited. But he said nothing.

"'You know, Sire, you are supposed to speak first.'

"'Oh, am I?' he said, and smiled. 'Well then, suppose we sit down.'"

King Albert of the Belgians.
Library of Congress, LC-DIG-hec-04612

The United States and the German Invasion of Belgium

During the early days of World War I, when it seemed that the Germans would win the war quickly, the government of Belgium sent representatives to the United States to alert President Wilson of the atrocities being committed against Belgian civilians. They hoped the United States would agree to pressure Germany into preserving Belgian independence following the war's end instead of allowing Germany to permanently occupy or partition it. Wilson refused to take sides, believing that his ability to negotiate a postwar peace between the combatant nations depended on his remaining neutral, even diplomatically, which he did until the United States joined the Allies in 1917. But even then, the story of Belgium's brutal occupation by the Germans during the war was viewed by outsiders as an exaggeration, even by Belgium's allies, who managed to carve out much more money for themselves in terms of postwar reparations than they did for Belgium. Belgium's economy never completely recovered, and the extent of German brutality against it was never fully believed, a fact that helped temporarily hide Nazi war crimes during World War II: reports of the existence of concentration camps were at first considered rumors as false and wild as the Belgian claims of German atrocities during World War I had been.

When Mary told King Albert—whom she described later as "a very big . . . blond young man, very patient, very worn"— why she had requested an interview, he said that he had already sent a "long message" to America. Then he mentioned his gratitude for what America had already done for Belgium by way of the American relief committees, which had provided food for the destitute occupied Belgian population.

When she asked him about the reported atrocities committed by German soldiers against Belgian civilians, he said that "it would be unfair to condemn the whole German army. Some regiments have been most humane, but others have behaved very badly." Mary asked him if the official Belgian reports on the invasion had been verified as fact. The king told her that the Belgian government had hundreds of journals from dead or imprisoned German soldiers that proved the truth of German atrocities on Belgian civilians.

Then the king confirmed a story that Mary had heard regarding the advancing Germans using Belgian civilians as human shields. "It is quite true," said the king, when Mary asked him about it. "When the Belgian soldiers fired on the enemy they killed their own people. Again and again innocent civilians of both sexes were sacrificed to protect the invading army during attacks."

Mary had been told that the interview would last 10 minutes, but she and King Albert spoke together for more than an hour. When Mary's typed transcription of the interview was formally approved by the king, Mary realized that she had a very significant document in her hand. She immediately mailed it to the United States, hoping that it would help counteract the German propaganda in America regarding the invasion and occupation of Belgium and help budge President Wilson's staunch diplomatic neutrality.

Unfortunately, the statement didn't have this desired effect: Germany continued its vicious occupation, and President Wilson refused to pressure them to stop. And although no further war interviews would compare, in Mary's opinion, with that of King Albert, before she left Europe she also met and interviewed two queens—Elizabeth of the Belgians and Mary of Great Britain—as well as important Allied leaders such as French general Ferdinand Foch and Winston Churchill (then the British lord of the admiralty).

When she returned home, Mary wrote 10 articles based on her observations and interviews that boosted readership of the *Saturday Evening Post* by 50,000. Afterward, the articles were also published in the *London Times* before they were collected into a book called *Kings, Queens and Pawns: An American Woman at the Front.*

Mary believed that the Allies would soon defeat Germany and that America would not have to enter the war. But the conflict lasted much longer than she—and most people—expected. When the United States declared war on Germany two years later, Mary—now not only a popular writer but also, after her travels on the western front, a celebrity—was asked by the editor of the *Saturday Evening Post* to write something that would influence American mothers to willingly send their sons to the war.

She was torn. While she believed that Germany needed to be stopped, her oldest son was now eager to join the military, and she had seen firsthand the gruesome effects of war on young men. So in an "agony of spirit" she locked herself in her writing office. After 12 hours she emerged with "The Altar of Freedom," an article that, when published, had the desired impact upon American mothers. But after she received hundreds of postwar letters from mothers who had lost their sons in the war, Mary deeply regretted having written it.

This regret caused Mary to take a pacifist stance during the early days of World War II. But by 1940 she had changed her mind. She felt that the United States needed to support Britain against Germany. In order to persuade her countrymen to do this, she asked the editor of the *Saturday Evening Post* if he would send her to Britain to report on the Blitz, to "tell people what the Germans are doing."

However, her grown sons discovered her plan and persuaded her to cancel it: she now had a heart condition, and the difficult travel arrangements necessary to get her to London during wartime would have seriously threatened her health. After Japan attacked Pearl Harbor, Mary—still a best-selling author—settled for working as an air raid warden and writing short but influential articles designed to encourage her fellow Americans to support the war effort.

She died in New York City in 1958 at the age of 82.

LEARN MORE

Improbable Fiction: The Life of Mary Roberts Rinehart by Jan Cohn (University of Pittsburgh Press, 1980).

Kings, Queens and Pawns: An American Woman at the Front by Mary Roberts Rinehart (George H. Doran Company, 1915).

My Story by Mary Roberts Rinehart (Farrar and Rinehart, 1931).

MADELEINE ZABRISKIE DOTY

"Germany Is No Place for a Woman"

"I packed my bags with a beating heart. Go I would—for why live unless adventure?"

> —Madeleine Zabriskie Doty on her
> decision to enter wartime Germany

Madeleine Zabriskie Doty was an attorney and journalist so committed to American prison reform that she had spent some time undercover in a women's prison to observe conditions firsthand. She wrote later that when she heard the news, less than one year later, that Europe was at war, "all my dreams

Madeleine Zabriskie Doty during the war.
Smith College Archives

for a better world came tumbling down like castles in the air. What was the good of working for prison reform when the world was on fire?"

She joined the American delegation of the International Congress of Women at The Hague in the Netherlands, as a correspondent for the *New York Evening Post*. As the meetings progressed and as women prepared to take their peace initiative around the world, Madeleine parted company with them. Although she wholeheartedly agreed with their purpose, she had discovered a purpose of her own: the *New-York Tribune* had commissioned her to report on wartime Germany. Officials at the American embassy at The Hague tried to change her mind, warning her that her timing was bad and that Americans were not welcome in Germany. The *Lusitania*—a British ocean liner that had sailed from New York with Americans on board—had just been sunk by the Germans. Plus, Madeleine had never been to Germany and didn't even speak the language. But she would not be dissuaded. She found a temporary traveling companion who spoke both German and English, removed the little American flag pin from her jacket, and in June 1915 set off for Germany's capital city of Berlin.

Most of the Berliners she saw were either goose-stepping soldiers or civilians in mourning, identified by their black arm bands, many of them deep in conversation. Madeleine could often overhear the word *Lusitania*. She received many threatening glares when her whispered English conversations with her companion were occasionally overheard.

Before her companion traveled on, she helped Madeleine find some people with whom she could stay: a frail middle-aged German university professor—who was scheduled to shortly report for military duty despite his poor health—and his American wife. They treated Madeleine well, but she was forced to

The *Lusitania* and the Naval Wars

After years of prewar tension between Great Britain and Germany regarding Germany's attempt to build a navy as large as Great Britain's, the opening of the Great War saw an actual naval war erupt between the two nations, a slightly different type than Germany had expected. Great Britain began a naval blockade to prevent German ships' access to the Atlantic Ocean. Ships attempting to sail from the Atlantic to German ports—even those importing food for civilians—were also blocked in hopes that Germany would soon surrender. But Germany fought back. Germany eventually realized that the only way to achieve naval dominance over Britain—and an aggressive way to fight the blockade—would be to conduct unrestricted submarine warfare. This meant torpedoing all merchant ships sailing to and from Great Britain without warning or concern for the loss of life (as opposed to following the rules of warfare, which allowed time for passengers of a doomed ship to get into lifeboats).

When the passenger liner the *Lusitania*, sailing from the United States to Liverpool, was torpedoed on May 7, 1915, off the coast of Ireland by a German submarine without warning, more than 1,000 civilians were killed, 128 of them Americans. The Germans claimed they had proof that the ship had been carrying Canadian soldiers and munitions. Still, the American outrage that followed caused Germany to temporarily cease unrestricted submarine warfare. But the British blockade of Germany continued throughout the war, causing immense suffering to the German population.

endure endless conversations in which her hosts praised Germany, criticized the United States, and justified the sinking of the *Lusitania*. "Better a thousand times that the *Lusitania* be sunk and Americans killed," they would say, "than let American bullets reach the Allies to inflict death on German soldiers."

Madeleine was determined to find Germans who wanted peace. Since her hosts wouldn't associate with such people and since she was required to report her every move to them, she obtained an address from a friend at the American embassy. One day, telling her hosts that she had a luncheon date, she got into a cab and found some German women referred to as Social Democrats who were meeting in secret. They told Madeleine about their hero, Rosa Luxemburg, who had been arrested after she had dashed out into a street filled with soldiers, shouting, "Don't go to war! Don't shoot your brothers!" Placed in solitary confinement by German officials, Rosa continued to be a source of inspiration to these women.

A few months after Rosa's arrest, hundreds of Social Democrat women marched on the Reichstag—the building that housed the German government—shouting, "We will have no more war. We will have peace!" The police quickly dispersed the women, ordering the newspapers to print nothing of the incident. Madeleine later wrote: "The task of peace propaganda in Germany is gigantic. Neither by letter nor by press can news be spread. Both are censored. The work must be carried on by spoken word, passed from mouth to mouth. The courage of the little band of women I had met was stupendous. Through them I learned to love Germany."

Madeleine then left Germany, but after spending some time in France and Great Britain, she was asked to return to Germany to report for the *New-York Tribune* and the *Chicago Tribune*. "We want the truth," said her editor. "You're a neutral, you want

Rosa Luxemburg

When Rosa Luxemburg, a Polish Jew who was a brilliant writer and speaker, moved to Berlin in 1898, she quickly became an international celebrity within the ranks of the German Social Democratic Labor Party (the Sozialdemokratische Partei Deutschlands or SPD)—at the time the most powerful socialist party in Europe. When Germany began preparing for war, Rosa was arrested for urging German workers to protest the coming conflict that would divide them from the working men of other nations. And when the SPD supported the war, she helped form the Spartacus League, which organized antiwar activities. Rosa spent most of the war in prison without trial: the German government officially considered her a dangerous agitator "with no regard for the interests of the fatherland." Vladimir Lenin admired Rosa's intellect, but she ultimately disagreed with him and wrote a powerful 60-page pamphlet—which Lenin tried to have destroyed—criticizing the Russian Revolution because she realized that it never intended to bring democracy and freedom to the working class. After being released from prison at the war's end, Rosa founded the Communist

Party of Germany and became embroiled in the postwar German revolution before she was murdered by German military police on January 15, 1919.

Rosa Luxemburg.
Library of Congress, LC-USZ62-122266

peace; we think you'll tell it." Although Madeleine was definitely nervous about returning to Germany, exposing the truth was something she could not resist. When she met an American friend on a stop in Denmark, he warned her to turn back. "America forgets that Europe is at war," he said, "and Germany is no place for a woman."

Madeleine didn't heed his warning. While in Berlin this second time, Madeleine saw intense hunger all around her and began to doubt that the Allied blockade of Germany would help defeat the country. "It is foolish to starve out Germany," she wrote. "This procedure does not hurt the governing classes and the rich. They will not suffer until the rest of Germany is dead. Starvation kills off the poor, but leaves the militarists intact." She believed that if the Allies would end the embargo and feed the German people, the Germans would rise up against their government.

When Madeleine visited a friend at the American embassy in Berlin, he warned her to leave, that her presence would make trouble for them at the embassy. "I shall . . . break no rules, cause no trouble," she replied, "but I'm in search of the truth, and as a free American citizen I mean to talk to every one I can from the Kaiser to Liebknecht [a vocal peace activist and cofounder, after the war, with Rosa Luxemburg, of the German Communist party]." Her friend, joking that he thought the kaiser would be safer than Karl Liebknecht, warned her again that she would be watched constantly.

He was right. "The funny thing about German spies," Madeleine wrote, "is that they dress for the part. They are as unmistakable as Sherlock Holmes. They nearly always wear gray clothes, a soft gray hat, are pale-faced, shifty-eyed, smooth-shaven, or have only a slight moustache, and carry canes."

One night, Madeleine and a new companion, a German woman who was a Social Democrat, gave the spies a chase all through Berlin. "We jumped from one car to another. It proved an exciting game. Once we went up to a gray-clad man, and asked him if he wasn't tired. But spies grow angry when spoken to. German officials have no sense of humor. If they had, I wonder if there would have been a war."

But constantly being followed eventually took its toll. Madeleine wrote, "I feel exactly as though I am in prison. I acquire the habit of looking out of the corner of my eye and over my shoulder. These spies are as annoying to their countrymen as to me. The people detest them. They grow restless under such suppression. Free conversation is impossible, except behind closed doors. Everywhere are signs 'SOLDATEN—VORSICHT BEI GESPRÖCHEN SPIONENGEFAHR' ('SOLDIERS—CAUTION WHEN SPEAKING. DANGER OF SPIES')."

In September 1916, Madeleine joined an international group of journalists who had been invited to an official tour of Germany. During a stop at the beautiful city of Baden Baden, only two things reminded Madeleine that Germany was at war. The first was the faint echo of cannons heard from across the French border. The second was a comment Madeleine overheard one of her guides say to another: "Never let her out of your sight."

While in Munich, a conversation with a hotel chambermaid made Madeleine realize how much the rest of Germany—in this case, one Bavarian—resented the Prussians dominating the other German states. "A curse on 1870," she said. "It was a sad day for Bavaria when she tied up with Prussia. They are bleeding our country to death. Twice as many Bavarians have been killed as Prussians. We have the worst of the fighting. . . . [The Prussians] are taking our food from us. . . . I am not a Social Democrat, but I'm beginning to feel they are right."

Madeleine met more Social Democrats while she was in Munich, those of the moderate branch of the party whose public

Prussia and the Unification of Germany

"The Saxons hated the Prussians & many Saxons said they & we ought to be on the same side."

—British soldier after speaking with a German from Saxony during the Christmas Truce of 1914.

During the 19th century, Germany was a group of 27 separate kingdoms, duchies, and territories, including Prussia, Bavaria, Saxony, Baden, and Hesse. Prussia was by far the largest and the most militarily minded of all the German kingdoms and when Germany became unified in 1871, the Prussian character began to exert its influence on the rest of Germany. At the time of World War I, the unification was still only decades old, and there was resentment throughout Germany at the direction in which the Prussians were taking the rest of the country.

meetings were tolerated in Bavaria with some restrictions. At one of their large public meetings Madeleine heard one of the Social Democrats speak passionately for peace to enthusiastic applause.

But before leaving Germany, Madeleine wanted to hear another German, one of Germany's most famous, speak about the need for peace. Clara Zetkin was a close associate of Rosa Luxemburg and Karl Liebknecht, as well as a leader in the Social Democratic Party and a supporter of women's rights, who had been instrumental in initiating the idea of International

Women's Day. She had been thrown in jail for being involved in antiwar activities, but now, because of poor health, she was being held under house arrest in Stuttgart.

Madeleine and her companion made the four-hour trip to Stuttgart without taking any luggage so they wouldn't arouse any suspicion. They intended to just visit and then leave the same night, but it was raining so hard that Clara convinced them to stay the night with her. "She is like a blazing comet," Madeleine wrote later, after hearing Clara speak. "Over sixty, white hair and shaken with illness, she fights on." Madeleine felt that now she had seen the best of Germany. "In the morning I might be arrested," she wrote, "but for the moment I didn't care. . . . If all this passionate energy breaks through Prussian organization, what a Germany it will be."

Before crossing the German border into Switzerland, the German military authorities seized all of the official German propaganda materials that Madeleine and the other journalists had been given by the German civil authorities. This made Madeleine realize that she would have to hide all the notes she had taken. She copied them onto tissue paper and hid them inside the lining of her coat. She was detained by German officials who carefully searched the contents of her suitcase—but her notes went undiscovered.

When she returned to the United States, Madeleine turned these notes into a series of articles that ran in a number of major newspapers and journals before being collected into a book titled *Short Rations: An American Woman in Germany, 1915–1916.*

Madeleine left the United States again to report on Russia, reaching Petrograd just three days after the Bolsheviks took over the government and staying there two months before traveling on to other countries.

After the war Madeleine worked tirelessly in numerous international activities, including serving on a committee for the League of Nations. In 1938 she initiated a program designed to prepare and educate young Americans for international work, Junior Year in Geneva, a program that continues to this day. Madeleine received a doctorate degree in political science from a university in Geneva, Switzerland. She lived there, for the most part, teaching and writing until her death at the age of 86 in 1963.

LEARN MORE

One Woman Determined to Make a Difference: The Life of Madeleine Zabriskie Doty edited by Alice Duffy Rinehart (Lehigh University Press, 2001).

Short Rations: An American Woman in Germany, 1915–1916 by Madeleine Zabriskie Doty (Century Company, 1917).

EPILOGUE

///

"We shall live all our lives under the shadow of this war."

—Elsie Inglis, Scottish surgeon

"I believe [posterity] will be completely unable to gauge the unspeakable suffering this war has brought."

—Käthe Russner, German surgical nurse

At 11:00 AM on November 11, 1918, Vera Brittain heard guns being fired at regular intervals, signaling to Londoners that the war was over. Later that evening, a group of her fellow VAD nurses convinced her to accompany them as they joined the jubilant crowds that were swarming the streets. The young nurses, wearing their Red Cross uniforms, cheerfully accepted the wildly enthusiastic congratulations of strangers, but Vera, feeling out of place amid the celebration, left and walked slowly back to her living quarters.

Writing later, she said of that moment: "For the first time, I realised, with all that full realisation meant, how completely everything that had hitherto made up my life had vanished with Edward and Roland, with Victor and Geoffrey. The War was over; a new age was beginning; but the dead were dead and would never return."

Vera's beloved brother Edward Brittain, her fiancé Roland Leighton, and her close friends Victor Richardson and Geoffrey Thurlow had all been killed in the war. The deaths of these four young men had broken Vera Brittain's heart. If only one of them had survived, there would have been someone with whom she could have remembered the others. But Vera was left alone to remember them all, desperately regretting her own initially enthusiastic support of the war that had killed the four people she had loved most.

When she published her memoir of the war years in 1933, titled *Testament of Youth*, she was able to clearly articulate the emotional pain the war had caused her, it immediately sold thousands of copies in Great Britain because it struck a chord with those who had also lost loved ones. More than 800,000 British servicemen had been killed in the war. Most, if not all, of them had left behind those who would never recover from their loss.

"Stretching across the earth from America to Russia, from Flanders to Gallipoli, were the hidden whitening bones of a generation of men."

—Vera Brittain, from *Honourable Estate* (1936)

The pain and loss suffered by Vera Brittain and the British people were like a shock wave that covered the majority of the globe. Approximately 10 million fighting men had been killed between August 1914 and November 1918. The young men who had survived, made suddenly old by the loss of limbs, eyesight, and sanity (and, in thousands of especially gruesome cases, their entire faces), would be living reminders of the war's human cost for decades to come.

Millions of women had been killed during the war as well: resisters and medical personnel killed in the line of duty, civilians who lived too close to war zones or who died from malnourishment due to wartime shortages, munitions factory workers who lost their lives in accidents, and those killed deliberately and systematically in mass murders such as the Armenian genocide, executions of Belgian and French civilians, and anti-Jewish pogroms during the Russian Civil War.

The women who survived found their lives significantly changed during the postwar turmoil. Some of those changes were for the better, while many were for the worse. Millions of war widows—many made homeless—struggled alone to raise families in the midst of war-devastated economies. Others would never be able to marry and have children because too many men of their own generation had been killed. Numerous workingwomen lost their jobs either because the munitions factories that had employed them closed or because returning veterans wanted their civilian jobs back.

"The temperature has fallen considerably during the last weeks. Heating of the living rooms has been forbidden by the authorities. A new struggle, which we were spared during the War, is being imposed upon us housewives: the struggle against the winter cold in our homes."

—Anna Eisenmenger, Austrian widow and mother, diary entry for November 20, 1918

Both men and women survivors now reconsidered the motivations that had once led them to support the war whole-heartedly. The universal motivation summarized in the often-used British wartime catchphrase "For king and country" now seemed to mock them. For many it seemed clear that no king and no country had been worth the enormous suffering caused by the war. The world map was redrawn as disputed borders between nations were altered. Colonists began to speak more openly of independence. And centuries-old dynasties—along with their royal families—were swept away and replaced by new governments and new nations, many of them simmering with new ethnic tensions and civil wars.

Members of the Russian royal family, who were murdered by the Bolshe-viks during the Russian Revolution. *Library of Congress, LC-DIG-ggbain-14685*

"We are facing such extraordinary, complicated problems. I am very consciously a Sovereign, and I fully realize that our class is going to have a difficult position in this wild rush for democracy."

—Queen Marie of Romania at the war's end

Many of these new nations obtained new citizens: during the immediate postwar years, women from many combatant countries received the right to vote. Even in nations where this didn't occur, such as Italy, France, and Turkey, women gained some new opportunities and a new visibility. Why? The war had given women all over the world a chance to prove themselves.

The American anti–female suffrage phrase "bullets for ballots" had been turned on its head, not only by Russia's inspiringly courageous Women's Battalion of Death (and other reports of female soldiers), which proved that women could participate in warfare if given the chance, but also by the significant and varied contributions many other women had made during the war. All of this loudly stated the obvious to many governments worldwide: it was time to treat women as citizens.

The women who had been involved in the war had another significant impact on the generation of women who came immediately after them, an impact that few would have predicted at the time but which was directly connected to how the Great War ended.

The Treaty of Versailles, written by Allied leaders during the Paris Peace Conference and signed by a representative of the German government—not the army, a point that would later become crucial—blamed Germany for initiating the invasion of Belgium and France. The war reparations that the Allies demanded Germany pay helped to cause severe economic hardship in a country whose people had already suffered extreme privations during the war. And in order to pressure German leaders to sign the treaty, the Allied embargo was kept in place until they did. Thousands of additional Germans starved to death during this time.

"We have made partners of the women in this war; shall we admit them only to a partnership of suffering and sacrifice and toil and not to a partnership of privilege and right? This war could not have been fought, either by the other nations engaged or by America, if it had not been for the services of the women—services rendered in every sphere—not merely in the fields of effort in which we have been accustomed to see them work, but wherever men have worked and upon the very skirts and edges of the battle itself."

—US president Woodrow Wilson, in a speech
given on September 30, 1918, urging Congress
to give American women the right to vote

The Germans were humiliated and angered not only by the treaty's harsh reparation demands but also by its terms that crippled the German military. Resentment against the Allies—especially France, whose officials had been most responsible for the treaty's severity—and political turmoil within its own borders raged in Germany for many years.

Then a former corporal who had been decorated for his work as a dispatch runner in the German army began to gain political prominence. He was persuasive and passionate when speaking on his favorite subject: how Germany—especially the German army—was not to blame for the war's outcome. Others were at fault, he said: the German communists and Jews who had been working for peace all throughout the war and had been, he claimed, working inside the government to bring it down. But he had a plan that would at last grant Germany its rightful dominant position in the world—the place that had been thwarted by the war's outcome—if only the Germans would trust him.

The man's name was Adolf Hitler.

The Second World War that he began created the need for a new generation of female heroes. Where could these women look for role models? The women of the previous war had by this time been largely forgotten. Although efforts had been made during the 1920s to memorialize the war's heroes, both men and women, with monuments, books, and films, most Europeans, impatient to forget the war, also forgot its heroes.

But now the memory of their courage was needed and eagerly recalled. Pearl Witherington, an agent sent into Nazi-occupied France by the Special Operations Executive, a British wartime organization, had been inspired to become involved in resistance work years before when she had read the biography of Louise de Bettignies.

Andrée de Jongh, a young Belgian woman from Brussels who created the successful escape line that rescued hundreds of Allied airmen from Nazi-occupied Europe, had grown up listening to her father tell her about the heroics of both Edith Cavell and Gabrielle Petit.

Nations that had employed women in supportive military positions during the First World War quickly opened their doors to them during the second: it had already been proven that women could make a highly valuable contribution by filling these roles. The United States and Britain both hired "land army" women to work the farms and female factory workers to manufacture war equipment during the Second World War, just as they had during the first.

Maria Bochkareva and her Battalion of Death had been written out of the Soviet history books because they had fought for the Provisional Government. But their courage under fire—and that of the women involved on both sides of the long Russian Civil War—was remembered when the new war began. Soviet women were given the most active official military role out of all the women in the combatant countries involved in World War II.

Ironically, the memory of the women heroes of World War I was largely eclipsed by the very women they had inspired. The more blatant evil enacted into law by Nazi Germany during the Second World War ensured that those who fought against it would continue to fascinate people long after the first war had become a vague, unpleasant memory—one brought to mind only by fading photographs of serious, helmeted young men standing in sandbagged trenches or smiling young women in ankle-length nursing uniforms, or by the presence of poppies in Remembrance Day ceremonies.

But the involvement of these forgotten women should secure for them a place in remembered history. During the conflict that was placed before them, they not only gained the gratitude of many in their own generation but they proved, for the first time on a global scale, the enormous value of a woman's contribution, paving the way for future generations of women to do the same.

ACKNOWLEDGMENTS

//

This book owes its existence to my editor Lisa Reardon, who thought that my writing a prequel to *Women Heroes of World War II* would be an excellent idea and who told me so repeatedly.

Once I finally saw the light, several people first ignited my enthusiasm, the most notable among them, Freddy Rottey of the Flanders Fields Museum at Ypres, Belgium, whose communications I found energizing and invaluable.

There are certain French books without which it would have been impossible for me to accurately tell the stories of three women contained in this book. Although there are several older English-language biographies of Louise de Bettignies, the best ones are in French, most notably *Louise de Bettignies* by René Deruk. The best information I was able to find on Emilienne Moreau was contained in Prof. Jean-Marc Binot's *Heroines de la Grande Guerre*, and I have relied heavily on his research. And for the material on Gabrielle Petit, I am indebted to Pierre Ronvaux and his excellent *Gabrielle Petit, la mort en face,* which not only straightens out the story from previous fanciful biographies but eloquently communicates the nuances of this fascinating woman.

I hope that some day English readers will have access to all these materials but thankfully I didn't have to wait, due to my husband John's ability to read French. I'm also indebted to him for his multiple French-language communications with Vincent Boez, Prof. Jean-Marc Binot, Bertin de Bettignies, Béatrice Parrain at the Musée de l'ordre de la libération, and Vincent Rédier, all of whom provided additional material and/or photographs. Eric Hamilton also provided assistance in this regard, so a special note of thanks is due him for being in Paris at an opportune moment.

Ecaterina Teodoroiu is another woman whose story could not have been included here without translation assistance, so I am grateful in this regard to Valeria Balescu, curator of the National Military Museum in Bucharest, Romania, who cheerfully provided me with photos and Romanian-language material, which was then translated beautifully into English by Neriah Cruceru.

Gratitude is due to the following people who agreed to review sections of the manuscript, for their helpful comments and encouragements: Dr. Allison Scardino Belzer, Rupert Colley, Louise Miller, Nick Miller, Freddy Rottey, and Dr. Meredith Veldman.

Finally, very special thanks are due to William A. Hoisington Jr., professor emeritus of modern European history at the University of Illinois at Chicago, for agreeing to read the entire manuscript and whose assessment was very encouraging.

GLOSSARY

///

artillery: weapons, including cannons, that fired exploding shells during World War I.

Balkan Wars: Two wars fought on the Balkan Peninsula in 1912 and 1913 involving Bulgaria, Serbia, Greece, Montenegro, Romania, and the Ottoman Empire.

Bolshevism: a Russian political faction led by Vladimir Lenin that deliberately started the Russian October Revolution; its Red Army fought the White Russian Army during the Russian Civil Wars and it eventually became the Communist Party of Russia.

cavalry: soldiers who do most of their fighting while on horseback.

Central Powers: When the war began, the Central Powers included Germany and Austria-Hungary, but as the war went on, other countries joined them as well.

eastern front: The area of fighting in Eastern Europe where troops from Austria-Hungary, Germany, and Bulgaria fought troops from Russia and Romania.

Franco-Prussian War: The war fought from 1870 to 1871 between independent German states (with Prussia in the lead) against France, the main outcomes being the unification of Germany and the German annexation of the French provinces of Alsace and Lorraine.

infantry: foot soldiers.

Kaiser Wilhelm: The monarch of Germany who was a close relation of King George V of England, Empress Alexandra of Russia, and King Albert of Belgium; the kaiser was obsessed with the idea of German dominance and lost his throne at the war's end.

King Albert: The king of Belgium who became a hero to the Allied cause when he denied the German army peaceful passage through Belgium on its way to Paris.

no-man's-land: First used during the middle ages to refer to disputed territory, the term was widely used during World War I—following the Christmas truce of 1914—to describe the area between the enemy trenches.

Paris Peace Conference: An international postwar meeting begun in January 1919, where the terms of peace—including the Versailles Treaty—and the new borders of many nations were decided by the victorious Allies.

Russian Revolution: The term for two events that took place during 1917—the February Revolution and the October Revolution—which resulted in the overthrow of the 300-year-old Romanov royal dynasty, Russia being taken out of the war, and the onset of the Russian Civil War.

shells: The explosive ammunition fired from artillery cannons.

shrapnel: Fragments that fly from an exploding artillery shell.

suffragettes: A term first used to mock members of the often-violent British suffrage organization, the Women's Social and Political Union; the label was eventually embraced by all women who were actively seeking the right to vote during the early part of the 20th century.

trenches: An enduring symbol of the stalemate of the war, especially on the western front, trenches were defensive—and in some cases, permanent—structures dug into the earth and built up to varying degrees where the fighting men lived and fought during the war.

Triple Entente: The name of the alliance begun in 1907 between Great Britain, France, and Russia—the three countries that declared war on the countries of the Central Powers in August 1914—and which was generally referred to as the Allied Powers or the Allies after the war began and as the war went on.

Tsar Nicholas II: Emperor of Russia, first cousin to King George of England and first cousin by marriage to Kaiser Wilhelm of Germany, who lost his throne and his life during the Russian Revolution.

western front: The area of fighting in France and unoccupied Belgium where Allied troops fought against the Germans.

NOTES

//

Epigraph

In valour, devotion to duty: Queen of Spies, 242.
I do not feel: Lines of Fire, 156.

Introduction

To-day has been far too exciting: Chronicle of Youth, 84.
Extracts from the writing of Vera Brittain are reproduced by
   permission of Mark Bostridge and T. J. Brittain-Catlin, liter-
   ary executors for the Vera Brittain Estate 1970.
Men whose mobilization: Condemned to Death, xi.
We are elated: With the Armies of the Tsar, 21.
In those days: Contacts and Contrasts, 21.
I was adamant: Lights Out, 10.
The [German] women: With Old Glory in Berlin, 71.
While the Italian: Lines of Fire, 121.
The [German] people: With Old Glory in Berlin, 131.
The memory of the Franco-Prussian War: Condemned to Death, ix.
I imagine that Austria will not: Hilltop on the Marne, 37–38.

Men from these nations fought: While much of the fighting on the eastern front took place in Poland, it was not technically a country at the time. During the war Poles were forced to fight one another when they were conscripted into the armies of Russia, Germany, and Austria-Hungary. Poland was given its independence and made into its own nation at the war's end.

Part I: Resisters

From the day when: War Memories, viii.
The fate: Lines of Fire, 17.
Nothing can describe: War Memories, 17.
The English spied: Spies of the First World War, 25.
invasion plots: Spies, 26–28.
causing the deaths of 50,000: Female Intelligence, 130.
spy "H-21": Female Intelligence, 129.
from nine all the way to 81: Spies, 162.
Shall this war of extermination go on?: Lines of Fire, 28.
I wish she wouldn't: To End All Wars, 45.
war corrupted motherhood: Women and the First World War, 87.

Edith Cavell

There are two sides to war: Souhami, *Edith Cavell,* 164.
three hospitals . . . 13 kindergartens: http://edithcavell.org.uk, Ryder, 72–73.
We wait for England: Ryder, *Edith Cavell,* 83.
Die Cavell müss: Silent in an Evil Time, 88; Ryder, *Edith Cavell,* 164.
If we are arrested: Souhami, *Edith Cavell,* 255.
I wish you hadn't: War Memories, 127.
Then we cannot: War Memories, 128.
conducting soldiers: Ryder, *Edith Cavell,* 180; Souhami, *Edith Cavell,* 326.
My aim: Souhami, *Edith Cavell,* 328.
her bright, gentle: Ryder, *Edith Cavell,* 213.
Standing as I do: Souhami, *Edith Cavell,* 372.

Don't think of me: http://edithcavell.org.uk.
Je meurs: Souhami, *Edith Cavell,* 377.
Germany has placed: Condemned to Death, 169.

Louise Thuliez

How mistaken: Condemned to Death, vii.
Don't worry: Condemned, xi.
We could not warn: Condemned, 53.
Madame LeJeune: Condemned, 111.
Endlich, endlich: Condemned, 112.
no "chief": Condemned, 135–136.
Because I am a Frenchwoman: Condemned, 136.
I am afraid: Condemned, 148.
far too proud: Condemned, 175.

Emilienne Moreau

six-foot-long cylinders: To End All Wars, 163.
strange beings: Héroines de la Grande Guerre, 114.
would have dispatched: Héroines de la Grande Guerre, 125.

Gabrielle Petit

Considering I have: Gabrielle Petit, 189.
helpful friend: Gabrielle Petit, 195.
We will be separated: Gabrielle Petit, 206.
At no time: Gabrielle Petit, 217.
My country!: Gabrielle Petit, 217.
I am Belgian: Gabrielle Petit, 250.
Just try it: Héroines de la Grande Guerre, 222.
I do not fear you: Héroines de la Grande Guerre, 224.
I will not: Héroines de la Grande Guerre, 224.

Marthe Cnockaert

Because I am a woman: I Was a Spy!, 8.
The Germans: I Was a Spy!, 11.

More than 1,000: Beauty and the Sorrow, 176.
Marthe, would you: I Was a Spy!, 39.
If my daughter: I Was a Spy!, 39.
A spy needs: I Was a Spy!, 44.
Already you have gained: I Was a Spy!, 157.
this was war: I Was a Spy!, 156.
I am going: I Was a Spy!, 161.
I look on myself: I Was a Spy!, 270–271.

Louise de Bettignies

We have thousands: Queen of Spies, 241.
Madame, before your foot: Résistante Lilloise, 99.
My child: Résistante Lilloise, 52.
I . . . was ready: Story of Louise de Bettignies, 50.
One just had to: Story of Louise, 51.
They are too stupid: Story of Louise, 78.
Bah! I know: Story of Louise, 86.
Danger does not . . . Yes, just like: Story of Louise, 93.
But we showed: Story of Louise, 142.
Until France: Story of Louise, 205.
The services: Story of Louise, 97.

Part II: Medical Personnel

Faster than . . . Short Rations, 56
Think of all the youth: Lines of Fire, 228.
fewer than 4,000 nurses: "Sisters of Mercy in Russia's Great War."
about 92,000 Germans: Women in the First World War, 39.
If we had been nursing: Alice Kitchen Diary, May 5, 1915.
This has been a dreadful: The War Diary of Clare Gass, 178–79.
The very word "wounded": Oceans of Love, 155.
These shells make: Field Hospital and Flying Column, 136.
shocking lot of casualties: Alice Kitchen Diary, May 6, 1915.
A very fierce German attack: Field Hospital and Flying Column,
    172.

Elsie Inglis

In Scotland they: The Quality of Mercy, 45.
done more: Elsie Inglis, 26.
My good lady: Dr. Elsie Inglis, 156.
The need is there: Elsie Inglis, 37.
But of course: Shadow of Swords, 153.
the enemy hospital: The Quality of Mercy, 161.
If it is a matter . . . make me: Shadow of Swords, 159.

Olive King

That first winter: Letters of Olive King, 20.
the third woman . . . the first woman: Letters of Olive King, 2.
send me a sorrow: Letters of Olive King, 2.
I sometimes feel: Letters of Olive King, 9.
in the thick of things: Letters of Olive King, 24.
making the workers feel: Letters of Olive King, 34.
I always feel: Letters of Olive King, 51.
soldiers from Serbia, France: The Beauty and the Sorrow, 331.
too dreadful: Letters of Olive King, 58.

Helena Gleichen

We are cleverer: Contacts and Contrasts, 192.
We are lucky: Contacts, 197.
Badly wounded men: Contacts, 243.
You can't pass: Contacts, 244.
as if [they] had been boys: Contacts, 21
very badly needed: Contacts, 125.
more than one million: Marie Curie and Her Daughters, 27.
no women: Contacts, 126.
suspiciously close: Contacts, 138.
not looking: Contacts, 190.
bustle and noise: Contacts, 208.
Soldiers here present: Contacts, 247.
Home Defence Corps: Contacts, x.

Shirley Millard

Banners streamed: Diary and Recollections of Shirley Millard, 1.

world must be made safe: Woodrow Wilson asking congress for a declaration of war against Germany, April 2, 1917. Woodrow Wilson Presidential eLibrary (woodrowwilson.org /library-archives)

We are all thrilled: Diary and Recollections, 3.

Inside, all was confusion: Diary and Recollections, 6–7.

Gashes from bayonets: Diary and Recollections, 8.

La gloire: Diary and Recollections, 9.

They were grinning: Diary and Recollections, 25.

Such gallantry: Diary and Recollections, 46.

somewhat wearily: Diary and Recollections, 48.

Bien, bien!: Diary and Recollections, 49.

My heart is sick: Diary and Recollections, 64.

a jumble: Diary and Recollections, 66.

someone good: Diary and Recollections, 68.

once again beating: Diary and Recollections, 68.

his friends and their mothers: Diary and Recollections, 68.

Part III: Soldiers

Once at the front: Lines of Fire, 155–56.

"Do you like short hair?": Red Heart of Russia, 106.

I want to shed: Lines of Fire, 20.

The dirt, the flies: Red Heart of Russia, 83.

I asked one man: Alice Kitchen Diary, entry for May 11, 1915.

They were not individual: Cossack Girl, 87.

women . . . in the armies of Austria-Hungary: Germany in Wartime, 280–81.

Close to 1,000 Russian women: They Fought for the Motherland, 30.

Women can fight: Red Heart of Russia, 114.

Is there any: American Women in World War I, 1.

Maria Bochkareva

The soul of the army: Red Heart of Russia, 107.
75 male officers and 300 fighting men: Yashka: My Life, 209.
Our soldiers were retreating: Yashka, 70.
Men and women citizens!: Yashka, 159–60.
a great human sacrifice: Red Heart, 101.
My reasons are so many: Red Heart, 101.
What else is left: Red Heart, 102.
Don't be cowards!: Yashka, 206.
Ha, ha! The women: Yashka, 211.
36 were wounded: They Fought for the Motherland, 111.
Good God! Women!: Motherland, 110.
battalion provided: Motherland, 111.
we were carried away: Red Heart, 110.

Flora Sandes

Little did I imagine: Autobiography of a Woman Soldier, 9.
duck to water: Fine Brother, 152.
Hourra! Hourra!: Autobiography of a Woman Soldier, 61.
tougher and more practical: Fine Brother, 36.
There are others: Fine Brother, 16.
Serbian soldier prides himself: Fine Brother, 44.
I don't like the thought: Fine Brother, 63
Nashi Engleskinja: Autobiography of a Woman Soldier, 14.
a most glorious moonlight night: An English Woman-Sergeant, 142–43.
Shut up: Fine Brother, 161.

Marina Yurlova

Adventure lay just ahead: Cossack Girl, 14.
To arms!: Cossack Girl, 7.
Who are you: Cossack Girl, 10.
Well, Marina: Cossack Girl, 34.
great black sea of men: Cossack Girl, 35.

Russia is asking: Cossack Girl, 46–47.
I'm a Cossack!: Cossack Girl, 47.
What's eating you: Cossack Girl, 64.
Here there was no question: Lines of Fire, 90.
being buried: Cossack Girl, 101.
had died for a cause: Cossack Girl, 117.
believed in any government: Cossack Girl, 140.
Brothers, I fought: Cossack Girl, 140–41.

Ecaterina Teodoroiu

She seemed a warrior child: Sublocotenentul Ecaterina Teodoroiu, 64.
To Jiu! To the bridge!: Sublocotenentul, 8.
complete the task: www.firstworldwar.com/source/romania
   _ferdinandprocl.htm.
The country is in danger: Sublocotenentul, 19.
Well done, my child: Sublocotenentul, 19.
true example for the soldiers: Sublocotenentul, 21.
If you care about me: "Copila zâmbitoare."
Move forward, boys!: Sublocotenentul, 53.
The second lieutenant girl has died!: Sublocontenentul, 53.
I should die of grief: The Last Romantic, 192.

Part IV: Journalists

Under certain conditions: Sapper Dorothy Lawrence, 42.
The few papers: War Memories, 8.
Whatever is printed: Germany in Wartime, 100.

Mary Roberts Rinehart

I am to go to the firing line: Diary I, Mary Roberts Rinehart papers.
I had at that time: My Life, 147.
appeal that [war] makes: Improbable Fiction, 80
Let me see: Kings, Queens and Pawns, 15.
details that meant nothing: Kings, 13.
everywhere: Kings, 16.

obsessed by the injustice: Kings, 49.

That is the thing: Kings, 103.

odour of that beautiful lagoon: Kings, 124.

shaking, rocking: Diary II, 100.

If a fusée goes up: My Story, 164.

I shone like a star: Diary II, 97.

No more gallant: Diary II, 100.

I advanced: My Story, 167.

a very big . . . blond young man: My Story, 167

long message: King Albert interview, Mary Roberts Rinehart papers.

it would be unfair: My Story, 168

It is quite true: Kings, 56.

agony of spirit: My Story, 221.

tell people what: Improbable Fiction, 225.

Madeleine Zabriskie Doty

I packed my bags: Short Rations, 26.

all my dreams: One Women Determined to Make a Difference, 123–24.

128 Americans: The First World War, 265.

Better a thousand times: Short Rations, 32.

Don't go to war: Short Rations, 37.

task of peace: Short Rations, 38.

with no regard for: Rosa Luxemburg, 210.

We want the truth: Short Rations, 83.

America forgets that: Short Rations, 90.

It is foolish: Short Rations, 116–117.

I shall . . . break: Short Rations, 120.

The funny thing about German: Short Rations, 120.

We jumped: Short Rations, 121.

I feel exactly: Short Rations, 122–23.

Never let her: Short Rations, 178.

curse on 1870: Short Rations, 204.

The Saxons hated: Silent Night, 123.

She is like a blazing comet: Short Rations, 226.

Epilogue

We shall live all our lives: Shadow of Swords, 97.

I believe [posterity] will be: Lines of Fire, 226.

For the first time: Testament of Youth, 463.

Stretching across the earth: Honourable Estate, 498.

The temperature has fallen: Lines of Fire, 297.

We are facing: Ordeal, 405.

We have made partners of the women: Woodrow Wilson Presidential eLibrary, www.woodrowwilson.org/library-archives.

BIBLIOGRAPHY

//

denotes those titles especially suitable for young readers

Books and Articles

Aldrich, Mildred. *A Hilltop on the Marne: Being Letters Written June 3–September 8, 1914.* New York: Grosset and Dunlap, 1915.

Badsey, Stephen. *The Franco-Prussian War 1870–1871 (Essential Histories).* Oxford, UK: Osprey, 2003.

Bailey Ogilvie, Marilyn. *Marie Curie: A Biography.* New York: Prometheus, 2011.

Bălescu, Valeria. "Copila zâmbitoare," *Observatorul militar* 36, September 10–16, 2002, Promemoria.

Balfour, Lady Frances. *Dr. Elsie Inglis.* New York: George H. Doran, 1919.

*Batten, Jack. *Silent in an Evil Time: The Brave War of Edith Cavell.* New York: Tundra Books, 2007.

Beatty, Bessie. *The Red Heart of Russia.* New York: Century, 1918.

Belzer, Allison Scardino. *Women and the Great War: Femininity under Fire in Italy.* New York: Palgrave MacMillan, 2010.

Berry, Paul and Mark Bostridge. *Vera Brittain: A Life.* London: Chatto and Windus, 1995.

Binot, Jean-Marc. *Héroines de la Grande Guerre.* Paris: Fayard, 2008.

Botchkareva, Maria, with Isaac Don Levine. *Yashka: My Life as Peasant, Exile, and Soldier.* London: Constable, 1919.

Braybon, Gail. *Women Workers in the First World War: The British Experience.* London: Croom Helm, 1981.

Brittain, Vera and Alan Bishop, eds. *Chronicle of Youth: Vera Brittain's War Diary, 1913–1917.* London: Victor Gollancz, 1981.

Brittain, Vera. *Honourable Estate: A Novel of Transition.* New York: Macmillan, 1936.

———. *Testament of Youth.* Great Britain: Victor Gollancz, 1933.

*Brown, Carrie. *Rosie's Mom: Forgotten Women Workers of the First World War.* Boston: Northeastern University Press, 2002.

Carter, Miranda. *George, Nicholas and Wilhelm: Three Royal Cousins and the Road to World War I.* New York: Random House, 2011.

Cohn, Jan. *Improbable Fiction: The Life of Mary Roberts Rinehart.* Pittsburgh: University of Pittsburgh Press, 1980.

Coulson, Major Thomas. *The Queen of Spies: Louise de Bettignies.* London: Constable, 1935.

d'Argoeuves, Hélene. *Louise de Bettignies.* Plon: 1937.

Darrow, Margaret H. *French Women and the First World War: War Stories of the Home Front.* Oxford: Berg, 2000.

De Croÿ, Princess Marie. *War Memories.* London: Macmillan, 1932.

Deruyk, René. *Louise de Bettignies Résistante Lilloise (1880–1918).* France: La Voix du Nord, 1998.

Doty, Madeleine Zabriskie. *One Woman Determined to Make a Difference: The Life of Madeleine Zabriskie Doty.* Edited by Alice Duffy Rinehart. Bethlehem, PA: Lehigh University Press, 2001.

Doty, Madeleine Zabriskie. *Short Rations: An American Woman in Germany, 1915–1916.* New York: Century, 1917.

Ellis, John. *Eye-Deep in Hell: Trench Warfare in World War I.* New York: Pantheon Books, 1976.

*Emling, Shelley. *Marie Curie and Her Daughters: The Private Lives of Science's First Family*. New York: Palgrave Macmillan, 2012.

Englund, Peter. *The Beauty and the Sorrow: An Intimate History of the First World War*. Translated by Peter Graves. New York: Alfred A. Knopf, 2011.

Ettinger, Elżbieta. *Rosa Luxemburg: A Life*. Boston: Beacon Press, 1986.

*Freedman, Russell. *The War to End All Wars*. New York: Clarion Books, 2010.

Gass, Clare. *The War Diary of Clare Gass, 1915–1918*. Edited by Susan Mann. Kingston, ON: McGill-Queen's University Press, 2000.

Gavin, Lettie. *American Women in World War I: They Also Served*. Niwot, CO: University Press of Colorado, 1997.

Gleichen, Helena. *Contacts and Contrasts*. United Kingdom: John Murray, 1940. Reprint, Kilkerran, Scotland: Mansion Field, 2013.

*Granfield, Linda. Illustrated by Janet Wilson. *In Flanders Fields: The Story of the Poem by John McCrae*. New York: Doubleday, 1995.

Grayzel, Susan R. *Women and the First World War*. New York: Pearson Education, 2002.

Grozea, Elsa. *Sublocotenentul Ecaterina Teodoroiu*. Bucharest, Romania: Editura Militară, 1967.

Higonnet, Margaret R., ed. *Lines of Fire: Women Writers of World War I*. New York: Plume, 1999.

Hochschild, Adam. *To End All Wars: A Story of Loyalty and Rebellion, 1914–1918*. New York: Houghton Mifflin Harcourt, 2011.

Jensen, Kimberly. *Mobilizing Minerva: American Women in the First World War*. Urbana: University of Illinois Press, 2008.

Keegan, John. *The First World War*. New York: Knopf, 1999.

King, Olive. *One Woman at War: The Letters of Olive King, 1915–1920*. Edited by Hazel King. Melbourne: Melbourne University Press, 1986.

Koenig, Marlene A. Eilers. *The Gleichens: The Unknown Royal Cousins.* Amazon Digital Services, 2012.

Krippner, Monica. *The Quality of Mercy: Women at War, Serbia, 1915–1918.* Newton Abbot, UK: David and Charles, 1980.

La Motte, Ellen N. *The Backwash of War: The Human Wreckage of the Battlefield as Witnessed by an American Hospital Nurse.* London: J. P. Putnam Sons, Knickerbocker Press, 1916.

Lawrence, Dorothy. *Sapper Dorothy Lawrence: The Only English Woman Soldier, Late Royal Engineers 51st Division, 179th Tunnelling Company, BEF.* London: John Lane, 1919.

Leneman, Leah. *Elsie Inglis: Founder of Battlefront Hospitals Run Entirely by Women.* Edinburgh: NMS Publishing, 1998.

Marie, Queen of Romania. *Ordeal: The Story of My Life.* New York: Charles Scribner's, 1935.

*Massie, Robert K. and Jeffrey Finestone. *The Last Courts of Europe.* New York: Vendome Press, 1981.

McAuley, Mary Ethel. *Germany in Wartime: What an American Girl Saw and Heard.* Chicago: Open Court Publishing Company, 1917.

McKenna, Marthe. *I Was a Spy!* New York: Robert M. McBride, 1933.

McLaren, Eva Shaw. *Elsie Inglis: The Woman with the Torch.* New York: Macmillan, 1920.

*McNab, Chris. *The World War I Story.* Gloucestershire, UK: History Press, 2011.

McPhail, Helen. *The Long Silence: Civilian Life Under the German Occupation of Northern France, 1914–1918.* London: I. B. Tauris, 1999.

Meyer, G. J. *A World Undone: The Story of the Great War, 1914–1918.* New York: Bantam Dell, 2006.

Millard, Shirley. *I Saw Them Die: Diary and Recollections of Shirley Millard.* Reprint, New Orleans: Quid Pro Books, 2011.

Miller, Louise. *A Fine Brother: The Life of Captain Flora Sandes.* London: Alma Books, 2012.

Mitchell, David. *Monstrous Regiment: The Story of the Women of the First World War.* New York: Macmillan, 1965.

Morton, James. *Spies of the First World War: Under Cover for King and Kaiser.* Kew, UK: National Archives, 2010.

Neiberg, Michael S. and David Jordan. *The Eastern Front 1914–1920: From Tannenberg to the Russo-Polish War.* London: Amber Books, 2008.

Oppenheimer, Melanie. *Oceans of Love: Narrelle—An Australian Nurse in World War I.* Sydney: Australian Broadcasting Corporation, 2006.

Pipes, Richard. *A Concise History of the Russian Revolution.* New York: Alfred A. Knopf, 1995.

Powell, Anne. *Women in the War Zone: Hospital Service in the First World War.* Gloucestershire, UK: History Press, 2009.

Proctor, Tammy. *Female Intelligence: Women and Espionage in the First World War.* New York: New York University Press, 2003.

*Rasmussen, R. Kent. *World War I for Kids.* Chicago: Chicago Review Press, 2014.

Rees, Peter. *The Other Anzacs: The Extraordinary Story of our World War I Nurses.* New South Wales: Allen and Unwin, 2008.

Reider, Antoine. *The Story of Louise de Bettignies* (English translation of *La guerre des femmes*). London: Hutchinson.

Roberts Rinehart, Mary. *Kings, Queens and Pawns.* New York: George H. Doran, 1915.

———. *My Story.* New York: Farrar and Rinehart, 1931.

Ronvaux, Pierre. *Gabrielle Petit, la mort en face.* Izegem, Belgium: Éditions Illustra, 1994.

Ryder, Roland. *Edith Cavell.* New York: Stein and Day, 1975.

Sandes, Flora. *An English Woman-Sergeant in the Serbian Army.* London: Hodder and Stoughton, 1916.

———. *The Autobiography of a Woman Soldier: A Brief Record of Adventure with the Serbian Army.* London: H. F. and G. Witherby, 1927.

Schneider, Dorothy and Carl J. Schneider. *Into the Breach: American Women Overseas in World War I*. New York: Penguin, 1991.

Souhami, Diana. *Edith Cavell*. London: Quercus, 2010.

Stoff, Laurie. "Sisters of Mercy in Russia's Great War." www .RussiasGreatWar.org.

Stoff, Laurie S. *They Fought for the Motherland: Russia's Women Soldiers in World War I and the Revolution*. Lawrence: University Press of Kansas, 2006.

Therese, Josephine. *With Old Glory in Berlin: The Story of an American Girl's Life and Trials in Germany and Her Escape from the Huns*. Boston: Page Company, 1918.

Thompson, Captain Donald C. *Blood Stained Russia*. New York: Leslie-Judge, 1918.

Thompson, Mark. *The White War: Life and Death on the Italian Front, 1915–1919*. London: Faber and Faber, 2008.

Thuliez, Louise. *Condemned to Death*. London: Methuen, 1934.

Thurstan, Violetta. *Field Hospital and Flying Column: Being the Journals of an English Nursing Sister in Belgium and Russia*. London: G. P. Putnam's Sons, 1916.

Torrey, Glenn E. *The Romanian Battlefront in World War I*. Lawrence, KS: University Press of Kansas, 2011.

Tuchman, Barbara W. *The Guns of August*. New York: Macmillan Publishing, 1962.

Weintraub, Stanley. *Silent Night: The Story of the World War I Christmas Truce*. New York: Free Press, 2001.

Wilson-Simmie, Katherine M. *Light's Out! A Canadian Nursing Sister's Tale*. Belleville, Ontario: Mika, 1981.

Yurlova, Marina. *Cossack Girl*. Somerville, MA: Heliograph, 2010. First published in 1934 edition by Macaulay.

Zuckerman, Larry. *The Rape of Belgium: The Untold Story of World War I*. New York: New York University Press, 2004.

Documents, Records, and Reports

Kitchen, Alice. Alice Kitchen Diary, Alice Kitchen Papers, Special Collections, State Library of Victoria, Melbourne, Victoria, Australia.

Roberts Rinehart, Mary. Mary Roberts Rinehart Papers, 1831–1970, SC.1958.03, Special Collections Department, University of Pittsburgh.

Websites

Edith Cavell: http://edithcavell.org.uk

The Great War Archives, University of Oxford: www.oucs.ox.ac.uk/www1/lit/gwa

Russia's Great War and Revolution: www.russiasgreatwar.org

A Multimedia History of World War I: www.firstworldwar.com

Woodrow Wilson Presidential eLibrary: www.woodrowwilson.org/library-archives/wilson-elibrary

INDEX